50 Kid Breakfast Recipes for Home

By: Kelly Johnson

Table of Contents

- Turkey and Cheese Roll-Ups
- Mini Pita Pizzas
- Chicken Quesadillas
- Veggie and Hummus Wraps
- Fruit and Yogurt Parfaits
- Ham and Cheese Pinwheels
- DIY Taco Cups
- Tuna Salad Stuffed Avocados
- Mini Meatball Subs
- Spinach and Cheese Stuffed Mushrooms
- Pasta Salad with Veggies
- Grilled Cheese and Tomato Soup
- Egg Muffins
- Chicken and Veggie Skewers
- Cheese and Cracker Kabobs
- Veggie-Stuffed Mini Muffins
- Greek Yogurt Chicken Salad
- Baked Chicken Tenders
- Veggie-Stuffed Quesadillas
- Homemade Chicken Nuggets
- Fruit Kabobs with Dip
- DIY Mini Sandwiches
- Sweet Potato Fries
- Broccoli and Cheese Stuffed Potatoes
- Corn and Black Bean Salad
- Mini Sliders
- Caprese Skewers
- Loaded Baked Potato Bites
- Roasted Chickpeas
- Sweet and Savory Rice Balls
- Ham and Pineapple Skewers
- Pasta and Veggie Soup

- Chicken Caesar Wraps
- Tuna Melt Sandwiches
- Veggie Sushi Rolls
- Breakfast Burritos
- Turkey and Veggie Muffins
- Cheesy Cauliflower Bites
- Fruit Smoothie Bowls
- Chicken and Rice Casserole
- Mini Veggie Frittatas
- Cheese-Stuffed Meatballs
- DIY Veggie Nachos
- Chicken and Spinach Pasta
- Mini Taco Bar
- Stuffed Bell Peppers
- Peanut Butter and Banana Roll-Ups
- Homemade Pizza Bagels
- Veggie-Packed Meatloaf
- Apple and Cheese Sandwiches

Turkey and Cheese Roll-Ups

Ingredients:

- 8 slices of deli turkey
- 4 slices of cheese (such as Swiss, cheddar, or your favorite)
- 1 tablespoon Dijon mustard or mayonnaise (optional)
- Lettuce leaves (optional)
- Pickles or cucumber slices (optional)

Instructions:

1. **Prep the Ingredients:** If using, spread a thin layer of Dijon mustard or mayonnaise on each slice of turkey.
2. **Layer Cheese:** Place a slice of cheese on top of each turkey slice. If you like, you can add a leaf of lettuce or a few pickle or cucumber slices on top of the cheese.
3. **Roll It Up:** Starting from one end, carefully roll up each turkey slice with cheese inside. If you've added extras like lettuce or pickles, make sure they stay in place as you roll.
4. **Slice and Serve:** Cut the rolls in half if you prefer smaller pieces, or leave them whole. Arrange on a plate and serve.

Tips:

- For extra flavor, you can add a thin layer of cream cheese or a sprinkle of herbs.
- These roll-ups can be made ahead of time and stored in the refrigerator for a quick lunch option.

Mini Pita Pizzas

Ingredients:

- 4 whole wheat or regular pita breads
- 1 cup pizza sauce
- 1 1/2 cups shredded mozzarella cheese
- 1/2 cup grated Parmesan cheese (optional)
- 1/2 cup sliced pepperoni or other toppings (e.g., mushrooms, bell peppers, olives, etc.)
- 1 teaspoon dried oregano or Italian seasoning
- Fresh basil leaves (optional, for garnish)

Instructions:

1. **Preheat Oven:** Preheat your oven to 400°F (200°C).
2. **Prepare Pitas:** Place the pita breads on a baking sheet.
3. **Add Sauce:** Spread a thin layer of pizza sauce over each pita.
4. **Add Cheese:** Sprinkle shredded mozzarella evenly over the sauce. If using, add a layer of grated Parmesan cheese.
5. **Add Toppings:** Add your desired toppings on top of the cheese.
6. **Season:** Sprinkle dried oregano or Italian seasoning over the top.
7. **Bake:** Bake in the preheated oven for 8-10 minutes, or until the cheese is melted and bubbly and the edges of the pitas are crispy.
8. **Cool and Serve:** Let the mini pizzas cool for a few minutes before cutting them into quarters. Garnish with fresh basil if desired.

Tips:

- You can customize these mini pizzas with various toppings based on your preferences.
- For a healthier version, use whole grain pitas and add extra veggies as toppings.

Chicken Quesadillas

Ingredients:

- 2 cups cooked, shredded chicken (grilled or rotisserie chicken works well)
- 1 cup shredded cheddar cheese
- 1 cup shredded Monterey Jack cheese
- 1/2 cup finely chopped bell peppers (any color)
- 1/2 cup finely chopped onions
- 1 tablespoon olive oil or butter
- 4 large flour tortillas
- 1 teaspoon ground cumin (optional)
- 1 teaspoon paprika (optional)
- Salt and pepper to taste
- Salsa, sour cream, or guacamole (for serving)

Instructions:

1. **Prepare Ingredients:** In a bowl, mix the shredded chicken with ground cumin, paprika, salt, and pepper if desired.
2. **Cook Veggies:** Heat 1 tablespoon of olive oil or butter in a skillet over medium heat. Add the chopped bell peppers and onions. Sauté for 3-4 minutes, or until the vegetables are tender.
3. **Assemble Quesadillas:** Lay a tortilla flat on a clean surface. Sprinkle half of one side of the tortilla with a layer of shredded cheddar cheese, followed by a layer of shredded Monterey Jack cheese. Add a portion of the cooked chicken and sautéed vegetables on top. Fold the tortilla in half.
4. **Cook Quesadillas:** Wipe out the skillet and add a small amount of oil or butter. Heat over medium heat. Place the folded tortilla in the skillet and cook for 2-3 minutes on each side, or until golden brown and the cheese is melted. Repeat with the remaining tortillas.
5. **Slice and Serve:** Remove from the skillet and let cool for a minute before slicing into wedges. Serve with salsa, sour cream, or guacamole.

Tips:

- For extra flavor, you can add a sprinkle of chili powder or fresh cilantro.
- Make these ahead of time and freeze them. To reheat, cook from frozen in a skillet over low heat until heated through.

Veggie and Hummus Wraps

Ingredients:

- 4 large whole wheat or regular tortillas
- 1 cup hummus (store-bought or homemade)
- 1 cup shredded carrots
- 1 cup sliced cucumber
- 1 cup cherry tomatoes, halved
- 1/2 cup sliced bell peppers (any color)
- 1/2 cup baby spinach or lettuce
- 1/4 cup thinly sliced red onion (optional)
- Salt and pepper to taste
- 1 tablespoon olive oil or balsamic vinegar (optional, for drizzling)

Instructions:

1. **Prep Ingredients:** Wash and slice all vegetables. If using, thinly slice the red onion.
2. **Spread Hummus:** Lay a tortilla flat on a clean surface. Spread a generous layer of hummus evenly over the entire surface of the tortilla.
3. **Layer Veggies:** Arrange the shredded carrots, sliced cucumber, cherry tomatoes, bell peppers, and baby spinach (or lettuce) in a single layer on top of the hummus. If using red onion, add it on top of the other vegetables.
4. **Season:** Sprinkle with a little salt and pepper. Drizzle with olive oil or balsamic vinegar if desired.
5. **Roll Wraps:** Carefully roll up the tortilla from one end to the other, tucking in the sides as you go to keep the filling contained.
6. **Slice and Serve:** Slice the wraps in half diagonally and serve immediately, or wrap them tightly in plastic wrap for a quick lunch on the go.

Tips:

- Feel free to customize with your favorite veggies or add ingredients like avocado or shredded cheese.
- For added protein, you can include cooked chicken or chickpeas.

Fruit and Yogurt Parfaits

Ingredients:

- 2 cups plain or vanilla Greek yogurt
- 1 tablespoon honey or maple syrup (optional, for sweetness)
- 1 cup granola
- 1 cup fresh berries (such as strawberries, blueberries, or raspberries)
- 1 banana, sliced
- 1/2 cup chopped nuts (such as almonds or walnuts, optional)
- Fresh mint leaves (optional, for garnish)

Instructions:

1. **Sweeten Yogurt:** If desired, mix honey or maple syrup into the Greek yogurt for added sweetness.
2. **Layer Parfaits:** In serving glasses or bowls, start by adding a layer of yogurt at the bottom.
3. **Add Granola:** Sprinkle a layer of granola over the yogurt.
4. **Add Fruit:** Add a layer of fresh berries and banana slices on top of the granola.
5. **Repeat Layers:** Repeat the layers of yogurt, granola, and fruit until the glass is filled, ending with a layer of fruit on top.
6. **Add Nuts (Optional):** Sprinkle chopped nuts over the top layer for added crunch and protein if desired.
7. **Garnish:** Garnish with fresh mint leaves if using.
8. **Serve:** Serve immediately or chill in the refrigerator until ready to eat.

Tips:

- You can customize the parfaits with different fruits and toppings according to your preferences and seasonal availability.
- For a dairy-free option, use coconut yogurt or almond yogurt and adjust the toppings accordingly.

Ham and Cheese Pinwheels

Ingredients:

- 4 large flour tortillas
- 1/2 cup cream cheese (softened)
- 1 tablespoon Dijon mustard (optional)
- 8 slices of deli ham
- 8 slices of cheese (Swiss, cheddar, or your favorite)
- 1/2 cup baby spinach or shredded lettuce (optional)
- 1/2 teaspoon dried Italian seasoning (optional)

Instructions:

1. **Prep the Tortillas:** Lay the flour tortillas flat on a clean surface.
2. **Spread Cream Cheese:** Evenly spread a layer of cream cheese over each tortilla. If using, spread a thin layer of Dijon mustard over the cream cheese.
3. **Layer Ham and Cheese:** Place 2 slices of ham on each tortilla, covering the cream cheese. Layer 2 slices of cheese on top of the ham. If using, add a layer of baby spinach or shredded lettuce.
4. **Season:** Sprinkle with dried Italian seasoning if desired.
5. **Roll Up Tortillas:** Carefully roll each tortilla tightly from one end to the other.
6. **Slice Pinwheels:** Using a sharp knife, slice each rolled tortilla into 1-inch pinwheels.
7. **Serve:** Arrange the pinwheels on a serving platter.

Tips:

- For a different flavor, you can use flavored cream cheese or add additional ingredients like pickles or sliced bell peppers.
- These pinwheels can be made ahead of time and stored in the refrigerator until ready to serve.

DIY Taco Cups

Ingredients:

- 1 pound ground beef or ground turkey
- 1 packet taco seasoning mix
- 1/2 cup water
- 8 small flour or corn tortillas
- 1 cup shredded cheddar cheese
- 1 cup shredded lettuce
- 1/2 cup diced tomatoes
- 1/2 cup sour cream
- 1/4 cup sliced black olives (optional)
- 1/4 cup sliced green onions (optional)
- Salsa or guacamole (for serving, optional)

Instructions:

1. **Preheat Oven:** Preheat your oven to 375°F (190°C).
2. **Cook Meat:** In a skillet over medium heat, cook the ground beef or turkey until browned. Drain any excess fat. Add the taco seasoning mix and water to the skillet and cook according to the seasoning packet instructions, typically for 5 minutes, until the mixture is well combined and heated through.
3. **Prepare Tortillas:** Using a round cutter or a glass, cut each tortilla into smaller circles (about 3 inches in diameter). You'll need about 2 circles per cup.
4. **Form Cups:** Press each tortilla circle into the cups of a muffin tin, creating a small cup shape. You can use the back of a spoon to help mold them.
5. **Bake Tortilla Cups:** Bake the tortilla cups in the preheated oven for 8-10 minutes, or until they are crispy and golden brown.
6. **Fill Cups:** Remove the tortilla cups from the oven and let them cool slightly. Spoon the seasoned meat into each cup, then top with shredded cheese. Return to the oven for an additional 2-3 minutes, or until the cheese is melted.
7. **Add Toppings:** Remove from the oven and let cool slightly. Top with shredded lettuce, diced tomatoes, sour cream, sliced black olives, and green onions as desired.
8. **Serve:** Serve the taco cups warm, with salsa or guacamole on the side if desired.

Tips:

- You can customize the fillings and toppings according to your preferences, such as adding beans or avocado.
- For a vegetarian version, replace the meat with black beans or sautéed veggies.

Tuna Salad Stuffed Avocados

Ingredients:

- 2 ripe avocados
- 1 can (5 oz) tuna, drained
- 2 tablespoons mayonnaise or Greek yogurt
- 1 tablespoon Dijon mustard (optional)
- 1 celery stalk, finely chopped
- 1/4 cup red onion, finely chopped
- 1 tablespoon fresh lemon juice
- 1 tablespoon chopped fresh parsley or dill
- Salt and pepper to taste
- Cherry tomatoes, halved (optional, for garnish)
- Lemon wedges (optional, for garnish)

Instructions:

1. **Prepare Tuna Salad:** In a bowl, combine the drained tuna, mayonnaise (or Greek yogurt), Dijon mustard (if using), celery, red onion, lemon juice, and chopped parsley or dill. Mix well. Season with salt and pepper to taste.
2. **Prepare Avocados:** Cut the avocados in half and remove the pits. If necessary, scoop out a bit of the flesh to create a larger cavity for the tuna salad.
3. **Stuff Avocados:** Spoon the tuna salad into each avocado half, filling the cavities generously.
4. **Garnish:** Top with cherry tomato halves if desired and garnish with extra parsley or dill. Serve with lemon wedges on the side if using.
5. **Serve:** Serve immediately for the best flavor and texture.

Tips:

- To prevent the avocado from browning, you can brush the cut surfaces with a little lemon juice.
- You can also add other mix-ins to the tuna salad, such as capers, chopped pickles, or a sprinkle of paprika for extra flavor.

Mini Meatball Subs

Ingredients:

For the Meatballs:

- 1 pound ground beef (or a mix of beef and pork)
- 1/4 cup bread crumbs
- 1/4 cup grated Parmesan cheese
- 1/4 cup chopped parsley
- 1 egg
- 2 cloves garlic, minced
- 1/2 teaspoon dried oregano
- 1/2 teaspoon dried basil
- Salt and pepper to taste

For Assembly:

- 6-8 small sub rolls or slider buns
- 1 cup marinara sauce
- 1 cup shredded mozzarella cheese
- 1/4 cup grated Parmesan cheese
- Fresh basil or parsley for garnish (optional)

Instructions:

1. **Preheat Oven:** Preheat your oven to 375°F (190°C).
2. **Make Meatballs:** In a large bowl, combine the ground beef, bread crumbs, Parmesan cheese, parsley, egg, garlic, oregano, basil, salt, and pepper. Mix until well combined. Form the mixture into 1-inch meatballs and place them on a baking sheet.
3. **Bake Meatballs:** Bake the meatballs in the preheated oven for 15-20 minutes, or until cooked through and browned on the outside.
4. **Heat Marinara Sauce:** While the meatballs are baking, heat the marinara sauce in a saucepan over medium heat.
5. **Prepare Sub Rolls:** Slice the sub rolls or slider buns in half, but not all the way through, leaving a hinge.
6. **Assemble Subs:** After baking, remove the meatballs from the oven. Place 2-3 meatballs in each sub roll. Spoon marinara sauce over the meatballs, then sprinkle with shredded mozzarella and grated Parmesan cheese.
7. **Melt Cheese:** Return the assembled subs to the oven and bake for an additional 5-7 minutes, or until the cheese is melted and bubbly.
8. **Garnish and Serve:** Garnish with fresh basil or parsley if desired. Serve warm.

Tips:

- You can make the meatballs ahead of time and freeze them for quick assembly later.

- Customize your subs with additional toppings such as sliced peppers, onions, or mushrooms.

Spinach and Cheese Stuffed Mushrooms

Ingredients:

- 12 large white or cremini mushrooms
- 1 tablespoon olive oil
- 1/2 cup finely chopped onion
- 2 cloves garlic, minced
- 2 cups fresh spinach, chopped
- 1/2 cup cream cheese, softened
- 1/2 cup shredded mozzarella cheese
- 1/4 cup grated Parmesan cheese
- 1/4 teaspoon dried oregano
- Salt and pepper to taste
- 2 tablespoons chopped fresh parsley (optional, for garnish)

Instructions:

1. **Preheat Oven:** Preheat your oven to 375°F (190°C).
2. **Prepare Mushrooms:** Wipe the mushrooms clean with a damp paper towel. Carefully remove the stems and set aside. Place the mushroom caps on a baking sheet, cavity side up.
3. **Cook Filling:** Heat olive oil in a skillet over medium heat. Add the finely chopped onion and cook for 3-4 minutes, or until softened. Add the minced garlic and cook for an additional 1 minute. Add the chopped spinach and cook until wilted, about 2 minutes. Remove from heat and let cool slightly.
4. **Make Stuffing Mixture:** In a bowl, combine the cooked spinach mixture with cream cheese, shredded mozzarella cheese, grated Parmesan cheese, dried oregano, salt, and pepper. Mix until well combined.
5. **Stuff Mushrooms:** Spoon the cheese and spinach mixture into each mushroom cap, packing it in slightly.
6. **Bake:** Bake the stuffed mushrooms in the preheated oven for 15-20 minutes, or until the mushrooms are tender and the topping is golden and bubbly.
7. **Garnish and Serve:** Garnish with chopped fresh parsley if desired. Serve warm.

Tips:

- For an extra touch, you can sprinkle a little extra Parmesan cheese on top before baking.
- You can prepare the stuffed mushrooms ahead of time and refrigerate them until you're ready to bake. Just add a few extra minutes to the baking time if they are cold from the fridge.

Pasta Salad with Veggies

Ingredients:

- 8 ounces (about 2 cups) pasta (such as rotini, penne, or farfalle)
- 1 cup cherry tomatoes, halved
- 1 cup diced cucumber
- 1/2 cup sliced black olives
- 1/2 cup diced bell peppers (any color)
- 1/2 cup shredded carrots
- 1/4 cup red onion, finely chopped
- 1/4 cup chopped fresh parsley or basil
- 1/2 cup crumbled feta cheese (optional)
- 1/4 cup grated Parmesan cheese (optional)

For the Dressing:

- 1/4 cup olive oil
- 2 tablespoons red wine vinegar or lemon juice
- 1 teaspoon Dijon mustard
- 1 teaspoon dried oregano
- 1 teaspoon garlic powder
- Salt and pepper to taste

Instructions:

1. **Cook Pasta:** Cook the pasta according to the package instructions until al dente. Drain and rinse under cold water to cool. Transfer to a large mixing bowl.
2. **Prepare Veggies:** While the pasta is cooling, prepare the vegetables. Dice the cucumber, slice the olives, chop the bell peppers, and finely chop the red onion.
3. **Mix Veggies and Pasta:** Add the cherry tomatoes, diced cucumber, sliced olives, diced bell peppers, shredded carrots, and red onion to the cooled pasta.
4. **Make Dressing:** In a small bowl, whisk together the olive oil, red wine vinegar (or lemon juice), Dijon mustard, dried oregano, garlic powder, salt, and pepper until well combined.
5. **Combine Salad:** Pour the dressing over the pasta and veggie mixture. Toss well to coat everything evenly.
6. **Add Cheese:** If using, gently fold in the crumbled feta cheese and grated Parmesan cheese.
7. **Chill and Serve:** Cover the salad and refrigerate for at least 30 minutes to allow the flavors to meld. Give it a final toss before serving and garnish with chopped fresh parsley or basil.

Tips:

- Feel free to add additional ingredients like cooked chicken, chickpeas, or artichoke hearts for extra protein and flavor.

- You can customize the salad with your favorite veggies or herbs based on what's in season or what you have on hand.

Grilled Cheese and Tomato Soup

Ingredients:

- 4 slices of bread (such as sourdough, whole wheat, or your favorite type)
- 4 slices of cheese (such as cheddar, American, or Swiss)
- 2 tablespoons butter
- Optional: 1-2 tablespoons mayonnaise (for spreading on the outside of the bread for extra crispness)

Instructions:

1. **Prepare Bread:** If using, spread a thin layer of mayonnaise on one side of each slice of bread. This will help the bread get extra crispy and golden.
2. **Assemble Sandwich:** Place a slice of cheese between two slices of bread, with the buttered or mayo side facing out. Repeat for the remaining sandwiches.
3. **Cook Sandwiches:** Heat a skillet or griddle over medium heat. Melt 1/2 tablespoon of butter in the skillet. Place the sandwiches in the skillet and cook for 3-4 minutes on each side, or until the bread is golden brown and the cheese is melted. Adjust the heat if necessary to avoid burning the bread before the cheese melts.
4. **Serve:** Remove from the skillet and let cool slightly before cutting in half. Serve warm.

Tomato Soup

Ingredients:

- 2 tablespoons olive oil
- 1 medium onion, finely chopped
- 2 cloves garlic, minced
- 1 can (14.5 ounces) diced tomatoes
- 1 can (6 ounces) tomato paste
- 2 cups vegetable or chicken broth
- 1 teaspoon dried basil
- 1/2 teaspoon dried oregano
- 1/2 teaspoon sugar (optional, to balance the acidity)
- Salt and pepper to taste
- 1/2 cup heavy cream or milk (optional, for a creamier texture)
- Fresh basil or parsley (optional, for garnish)

Instructions:

1. **Cook Vegetables:** Heat olive oil in a large pot over medium heat. Add the chopped onion and cook for 5 minutes, or until softened. Add the minced garlic and cook for another 1 minute.
2. **Add Tomatoes:** Stir in the diced tomatoes and tomato paste. Cook for 2-3 minutes, stirring occasionally.

3. **Add Broth and Seasonings:** Pour in the broth and add dried basil, oregano, and sugar if using. Bring to a simmer and cook for 15-20 minutes to allow the flavors to meld.
4. **Blend Soup:** For a smooth texture, use an immersion blender to puree the soup directly in the pot. Alternatively, carefully transfer the soup in batches to a blender and blend until smooth. Return to the pot if using a blender.
5. **Add Cream:** Stir in the heavy cream or milk if desired. Heat through but do not boil.
6. **Season and Serve:** Adjust seasoning with salt and pepper to taste. Garnish with fresh basil or parsley if desired. Serve hot with grilled cheese sandwiches.

Tips:

- For added flavor, you can sauté some diced carrots or celery with the onions.
- You can also add a splash of balsamic vinegar or a pinch of red pepper flakes to the soup for extra depth of flavor.

Egg Muffins

Ingredients:

- 6 large eggs
- 1/4 cup milk (any kind: whole, skim, almond, etc.)
- 1/2 cup shredded cheese (cheddar, mozzarella, or your favorite)
- 1/2 cup diced cooked ham, bacon, or sausage (optional)
- 1/2 cup diced bell peppers (any color)
- 1/4 cup diced onion
- 1/4 cup chopped spinach or kale
- Salt and pepper to taste
- 1/2 teaspoon dried herbs (such as oregano, thyme, or basil, optional)
- Non-stick cooking spray or a small amount of oil for greasing

Instructions:

1. **Preheat Oven:** Preheat your oven to 375°F (190°C). Grease a muffin tin with non-stick cooking spray or lightly oil it.
2. **Prepare Filling:** In a mixing bowl, combine the diced ham (or bacon/sausage), bell peppers, onion, and spinach. You can mix and match vegetables and proteins according to your preference.
3. **Mix Eggs:** In another bowl, whisk together the eggs, milk, salt, pepper, and dried herbs if using.
4. **Assemble Muffins:** Divide the vegetable and meat mixture evenly among the muffin cups. Pour the egg mixture over the filling in each cup, filling each about 3/4 full. Sprinkle shredded cheese on top.
5. **Bake:** Bake in the preheated oven for 20-25 minutes, or until the egg muffins are set in the middle and the tops are lightly golden.
6. **Cool and Serve:** Let the egg muffins cool for a few minutes before removing them from the tin. Serve warm, or store in an airtight container in the refrigerator for up to a week.

Tips:

- For added flavor, you can include ingredients like chopped tomatoes, mushrooms, or zucchini.
- Egg muffins can be made ahead of time and frozen. To reheat, simply microwave for about 1-2 minutes or until heated through.
- You can customize these muffins to fit dietary preferences by using egg substitutes, non-dairy milk, or different types of cheese.

Chicken and Veggie Skewers

Ingredients:

- 1 pound chicken breast or thighs, cut into bite-sized pieces
- 1 red bell pepper, cut into chunks
- 1 yellow bell pepper, cut into chunks
- 1 zucchini, sliced into rounds
- 1 red onion, cut into chunks
- 8-10 cherry tomatoes
- 1/4 cup olive oil
- 2 tablespoons soy sauce
- 2 tablespoons lemon juice or balsamic vinegar
- 2 cloves garlic, minced
- 1 teaspoon dried oregano or Italian seasoning
- Salt and pepper to taste
- Wooden or metal skewers (if using wooden skewers, soak them in water for 30 minutes to prevent burning)

Instructions:

1. **Prepare Marinade:** In a large bowl, whisk together the olive oil, soy sauce, lemon juice or balsamic vinegar, minced garlic, dried oregano or Italian seasoning, salt, and pepper.
2. **Marinate Chicken:** Add the chicken pieces to the marinade and toss to coat. Let it marinate for at least 30 minutes, or up to 2 hours in the refrigerator for more flavor.
3. **Prepare Vegetables:** While the chicken is marinating, cut and prepare your vegetables.
4. **Assemble Skewers:** Thread the marinated chicken pieces and vegetables onto the skewers, alternating between chicken and vegetables. Leave a little space between each item for even cooking.
5. **Preheat Grill or Oven:** If grilling, preheat your grill to medium-high heat. If using an oven, preheat to 400°F (200°C) and line a baking sheet with aluminum foil or parchment paper.
6. **Cook Skewers:**
    - **Grilling:** Grill the skewers for 10-15 minutes, turning occasionally, until the chicken is cooked through and has nice grill marks, and the vegetables are tender.
    - **Oven:** Arrange the skewers on the prepared baking sheet and bake for 20-25 minutes, or until the chicken is cooked through and the vegetables are tender, turning halfway through.
7. **Serve:** Remove the skewers from the grill or oven and let them rest for a few minutes. Serve warm.

Tips:

- For extra flavor, you can add a splash of lemon juice or a sprinkle of fresh herbs right before serving.

- Feel free to customize the vegetables based on what you have on hand or what's in season.
- If you prefer a spicier kick, add a pinch of red pepper flakes or use a spicy marinade.

Cheese and Cracker Kabobs

Ingredients:

- 1 cup cubed cheese (such as cheddar, Swiss, or Gouda)
- 1 cup sliced deli meats (such as salami, ham, or turkey), cut into bite-sized pieces
- 1 cup grape tomatoes or cherry tomatoes
- 1 cup cucumber slices or cherry tomatoes
- 1/2 cup black or green olives (optional)
- 1/4 cup sliced pickles or pickled vegetables (optional)
- 12-15 wooden skewers or toothpicks

Instructions:

1. **Prepare Ingredients:** Cube the cheese and cut the deli meats into bite-sized pieces. Slice the cucumber into rounds if using.
2. **Assemble Kabobs:** Thread a piece of cheese, followed by a piece of deli meat, then a tomato, and optionally an olive or pickle onto each skewer or toothpick. You can alternate and arrange the ingredients in any order you like.
3. **Serve:** Arrange the assembled kabobs on a platter. Serve immediately, or cover and refrigerate until ready to serve.

Tips:

- Customize the kabobs with your favorite cheeses and deli meats, or add extras like bell pepper slices or fresh herbs.
- For a festive touch, use holiday-themed or colored skewers or toothpicks.
- These kabobs are perfect for parties, picnics, or as a fun after-school snack.

Veggie-Stuffed Mini Muffins

Ingredients:

For the Muffins:

- 1 cup all-purpose flour
- 1 cup whole wheat flour
- 1 teaspoon baking powder
- 1/2 teaspoon baking soda
- 1/2 teaspoon salt
- 1/2 cup grated cheese (cheddar, mozzarella, or your choice)
- 1/2 cup finely grated or chopped veggies (carrots, zucchini, or bell peppers work well)
- 1/2 cup Greek yogurt or sour cream
- 2 large eggs
- 1/4 cup olive oil or melted butter
- 1/4 cup milk
- 1 tablespoon honey or maple syrup (optional, for a touch of sweetness)

For the Filling:

- 1/2 cup finely chopped spinach or kale
- 1/2 cup diced tomatoes (fresh or sun-dried)
- 1/4 cup finely chopped onions or scallions

Instructions:

1. **Preheat Oven:** Preheat your oven to 375°F (190°C). Grease a mini muffin tin or line it with mini muffin liners.
2. **Prepare Dry Ingredients:** In a large bowl, whisk together the all-purpose flour, whole wheat flour, baking powder, baking soda, and salt.
3. **Mix Wet Ingredients:** In another bowl, combine the Greek yogurt (or sour cream), eggs, olive oil (or melted butter), milk, and honey (if using).
4. **Combine Mixtures:** Add the wet ingredients to the dry ingredients and stir until just combined. Gently fold in the grated cheese and chopped veggies.
5. **Prepare Filling:** In a small bowl, mix together the chopped spinach, diced tomatoes, and chopped onions.
6. **Assemble Muffins:** Spoon a small amount of the muffin batter into each mini muffin cup, filling about halfway. Add a small spoonful of the veggie filling on top of the batter. Cover with additional muffin batter, filling each cup almost to the top.
7. **Bake:** Bake in the preheated oven for 12-15 minutes, or until the muffins are golden brown and a toothpick inserted into the center comes out clean.
8. **Cool and Serve:** Let the muffins cool in the tin for a few minutes before transferring to a wire rack to cool completely. Serve warm or at room temperature.

Tips:

- You can customize the muffins with any veggies you like or add herbs and spices for extra flavor.
- These mini muffins can be frozen and reheated in the microwave or oven for a quick snack.

Greek Yogurt Chicken Salad

Ingredients:

- 2 cups cooked chicken, diced or shredded (rotisserie chicken works well)
- 1 cup plain Greek yogurt (full-fat or low-fat)
- 2 tablespoons mayonnaise (optional, for extra creaminess)
- 1 tablespoon Dijon mustard
- 1 tablespoon lemon juice
- 1 celery stalk, finely chopped
- 1/2 cup diced red apple (optional, for a touch of sweetness)
- 1/4 cup chopped red onion
- 1/4 cup chopped fresh parsley or dill
- Salt and pepper to taste
- 1/4 cup chopped walnuts or almonds (optional, for added crunch)
- Lettuce leaves or whole-grain bread (for serving)

Instructions:

1. **Prepare Chicken:** If not using pre-cooked chicken, cook chicken breasts by poaching, grilling, or baking until fully cooked. Allow to cool, then dice or shred the chicken.
2. **Mix Dressing:** In a large bowl, combine the Greek yogurt, mayonnaise (if using), Dijon mustard, and lemon juice. Mix until smooth and well combined.
3. **Combine Ingredients:** Add the diced chicken, chopped celery, diced apple (if using), chopped red onion, and fresh parsley or dill to the bowl. Stir until all ingredients are well coated with the yogurt dressing.
4. **Season:** Season with salt and pepper to taste. If using, fold in the chopped walnuts or almonds for added texture.
5. **Chill and Serve:** Chill the chicken salad in the refrigerator for at least 30 minutes to allow the flavors to meld. Serve on a bed of lettuce, as a sandwich filling, or with whole-grain crackers.

Tips:

- You can customize the salad by adding other ingredients like grapes, chopped bell peppers, or a sprinkle of paprika.
- For extra protein, you can add a hard-boiled egg or some chickpeas.
- If you prefer a spicier kick, add a dash of hot sauce or a pinch of cayenne pepper to the dressing.

Baked Chicken Tenders

Ingredients:

- 1 pound chicken tenders or chicken breast cut into strips
- 1 cup buttermilk (or milk with 1 tablespoon lemon juice or vinegar)
- 1 cup panko breadcrumbs (for extra crunch)
- 1/2 cup grated Parmesan cheese
- 1 teaspoon paprika
- 1 teaspoon garlic powder
- 1/2 teaspoon onion powder
- 1/2 teaspoon dried oregano or thyme
- Salt and pepper to taste
- Non-stick cooking spray or a small amount of olive oil for greasing

Instructions:

1. **Preheat Oven:** Preheat your oven to 400°F (200°C). Line a baking sheet with parchment paper or lightly grease it with non-stick spray.
2. **Prepare Chicken:** If using chicken breasts, cut them into strips. Soak the chicken tenders in buttermilk for at least 30 minutes, or up to 2 hours in the refrigerator. This helps to tenderize the chicken and adds flavor.
3. **Prepare Breading:** In a shallow bowl, combine the panko breadcrumbs, grated Parmesan cheese, paprika, garlic powder, onion powder, dried oregano (or thyme), salt, and pepper.
4. **Coat Chicken:** Remove the chicken tenders from the buttermilk, allowing any excess to drip off. Dredge each tender in the breadcrumb mixture, pressing gently to adhere the crumbs. Arrange the breaded chicken tenders on the prepared baking sheet.
5. **Bake:** Lightly spray the tops of the chicken tenders with cooking spray or drizzle with a small amount of olive oil to help them crisp up. Bake in the preheated oven for 15-20 minutes, or until the chicken is cooked through and the coating is golden brown and crispy. The internal temperature of the chicken should reach 165°F (74°C).
6. **Serve:** Allow the chicken tenders to cool for a few minutes before serving. They are great with dipping sauces like honey mustard, barbecue sauce, or ranch dressing.

Tips:

- For added flavor, you can marinate the chicken in a mixture of buttermilk and spices overnight.
- If you prefer a spicier kick, add a pinch of cayenne pepper or chili powder to the breadcrumb mixture.
- To ensure the tenders are extra crispy, make sure they are not touching on the baking sheet, and avoid overcrowding the pan.

Veggie-Stuffed Quesadillas

Ingredients:

- 4 large flour tortillas
- 1 cup shredded cheese (cheddar, Monterey Jack, or a blend)
- 1 cup diced bell peppers (any color)
- 1 cup chopped spinach or kale
- 1/2 cup diced red onion
- 1/2 cup corn kernels (fresh, frozen, or canned)
- 1/2 cup black beans, drained and rinsed (optional)
- 1 tablespoon olive oil or butter
- 1 teaspoon ground cumin
- 1 teaspoon paprika
- Salt and pepper to taste
- Optional: 1/4 cup chopped cilantro or fresh parsley
- Optional: Sour cream, salsa, or guacamole (for serving)

Instructions:

1. **Prepare Veggies:** Heat a skillet over medium heat. Add a small amount of olive oil and sauté the diced bell peppers, chopped spinach or kale, diced red onion, corn, and black beans (if using). Season with ground cumin, paprika, salt, and pepper. Cook until the vegetables are tender, about 5-7 minutes. Remove from heat and set aside.
2. **Assemble Quesadillas:** Place one tortilla on a flat surface. Sprinkle half of the shredded cheese evenly over one half of the tortilla. Spoon half of the veggie mixture over the cheese. Sprinkle a little more cheese on top of the veggies to help the quesadilla stick together. Fold the tortilla in half to cover the filling.
3. **Cook Quesadillas:** Heat a large skillet over medium heat and add a little olive oil or butter. Place the folded quesadilla in the skillet and cook for 2-3 minutes on each side, or until the tortilla is golden brown and the cheese is melted. Repeat with the remaining tortillas and filling.
4. **Serve:** Remove the quesadilla from the skillet and let it cool for a minute before cutting it into wedges. Serve warm with sour cream, salsa, or guacamole if desired.

Tips:

- Feel free to customize the veggie filling with other ingredients such as mushrooms, zucchini, or tomatoes.
- For extra flavor, add a sprinkle of chili powder or a dash of hot sauce to the veggie mixture.
- You can also add cooked chicken or beef to the quesadillas for added protein.
- If you prefer a crispier texture, you can cook the quesadillas in a panini press or on a grill.

Homemade Chicken Nuggets

Ingredients:

- 1 pound chicken breast, cut into bite-sized pieces
- 1 cup all-purpose flour
- 2 large eggs
- 1 cup panko breadcrumbs (for extra crunch) or regular breadcrumbs
- 1/2 cup grated Parmesan cheese
- 1 teaspoon paprika
- 1 teaspoon garlic powder
- 1/2 teaspoon onion powder
- 1/2 teaspoon dried oregano or thyme
- Salt and pepper to taste
- Non-stick cooking spray or a small amount of olive oil for greasing

Instructions:

1. **Preheat Oven:** Preheat your oven to 400°F (200°C). Line a baking sheet with parchment paper or lightly grease it with non-stick spray.
2. **Prepare Breading Stations:** Set up three shallow bowls for breading:
   - **Flour Bowl:** Place the flour in the first bowl.
   - **Egg Bowl:** In the second bowl, beat the eggs.
   - **Breadcrumb Bowl:** In the third bowl, combine the panko breadcrumbs, grated Parmesan cheese, paprika, garlic powder, onion powder, dried oregano (or thyme), salt, and pepper.
3. **Bread the Chicken:**
   - Coat each piece of chicken in the flour, shaking off any excess.
   - Dip the floured chicken into the beaten eggs, allowing any excess to drip off.
   - Coat the chicken in the breadcrumb mixture, pressing gently to adhere the crumbs.
4. **Arrange on Baking Sheet:** Place the breaded chicken nuggets on the prepared baking sheet in a single layer. Lightly spray the tops with cooking spray or drizzle with a small amount of olive oil to help them crisp up.
5. **Bake:** Bake in the preheated oven for 15-20 minutes, or until the chicken is cooked through and the nuggets are golden brown and crispy. The internal temperature of the chicken should reach 165°F (74°C).
6. **Serve:** Allow the chicken nuggets to cool slightly before serving. They are great with dipping sauces like ketchup, honey mustard, barbecue sauce, or ranch dressing.

Tips:

- For a spicier version, add a pinch of cayenne pepper or red pepper flakes to the breadcrumb mixture.

- If you prefer to fry the nuggets, heat a few inches of oil in a deep skillet or fryer to 350°F (175°C) and fry the nuggets in batches until golden brown and cooked through. Drain on paper towels.
- You can freeze uncooked breaded chicken nuggets. Just arrange them in a single layer on a baking sheet, freeze until solid, then transfer to a freezer bag. Bake directly from frozen, adding a few extra minutes to the cooking time.

Fruit Kabobs with Dip

Ingredients:

For the Fruit Kabobs:

- 1 cup strawberries, hulled
- 1 cup pineapple chunks
- 1 cup seedless grapes
- 1 cup cantaloupe or honeydew melon, cut into cubes
- 1 banana, sliced (optional, but add just before serving to prevent browning)
- Wooden skewers or toothpicks

For the Dip:

- 1/2 cup plain Greek yogurt
- 2 tablespoons honey or maple syrup
- 1 teaspoon vanilla extract
- Optional: 1/4 teaspoon ground cinnamon or a pinch of nutmeg for added flavor

Instructions:

1. **Prepare Fruit:** Wash and prepare all fruit. Cut the strawberries in half if they are large. Cut the pineapple and melon into bite-sized chunks. If using banana, slice it just before assembling the kabobs to prevent browning.
2. **Assemble Kabobs:** Thread the fruit onto wooden skewers or toothpicks, alternating between different types of fruit. You can arrange them in any pattern or color combination you like.
3. **Prepare Dip:** In a small bowl, mix together the Greek yogurt, honey (or maple syrup), and vanilla extract. If desired, add ground cinnamon or a pinch of nutmeg for extra flavor.
4. **Serve:** Arrange the fruit kabobs on a platter and serve with the yogurt dip on the side.

Tips:

- You can customize the kabobs with your favorite fruits or whatever is in season.
- For an extra touch, sprinkle a little shredded coconut or chopped nuts on the dip.
- To make the dip a bit richer, you can use flavored Greek yogurt or add a spoonful of fruit preserves or jam to the mixture.
- If preparing ahead of time, keep the fruit kabobs refrigerated and assemble the dip just before serving to ensure freshness.

DIY Mini Sandwiches

Ingredients:

- 12 mini sandwich rolls or slider buns
- 1/2 cup mayonnaise or Greek yogurt
- 2 tablespoons Dijon mustard
- 1/2 pound sliced deli meats (turkey, ham, chicken, or roast beef)
- 1/2 pound sliced cheese (cheddar, Swiss, provolone, or your choice)
- 1 cup lettuce leaves (romaine, spinach, or mixed greens)
- 1 cup thinly sliced vegetables (tomato, cucumber, bell pepper, or pickles)
- 1/4 cup chopped fresh herbs (optional: basil, parsley, or chives)
- Salt and pepper to taste
- Optional: Sliced avocado, bacon strips, or olives

Instructions:

1. **Prepare Condiments:** In a small bowl, mix together the mayonnaise (or Greek yogurt) and Dijon mustard. You can also add a pinch of salt and pepper or other seasonings if desired.
2. **Assemble Sandwiches:**
   - Slice the mini rolls or slider buns in half.
   - Spread a thin layer of the condiment mixture on the inside of each roll.
   - Layer the deli meats, cheese, lettuce, and sliced vegetables on the bottom half of each roll. If using, add avocado slices, bacon strips, or olives for extra flavor.
3. **Add Herbs:** Sprinkle the chopped fresh herbs over the fillings for added freshness and flavor.
4. **Top and Serve:** Place the top half of the roll on each sandwich. Arrange the mini sandwiches on a platter. You can cut them in half diagonally for a more elegant presentation if desired.
5. **Serve:** Serve immediately, or cover with plastic wrap and refrigerate until ready to serve.

Tips:

- You can customize the mini sandwiches with different types of bread or rolls, including whole-grain, ciabatta, or pita.
- For a vegetarian option, use hummus as a spread and fill with roasted vegetables or extra cheese.
- To add a touch of sweetness, include a slice of apple or pear in the sandwiches.
- For a more substantial meal, add a layer of coleslaw or potato salad to the sandwiches.
- Mini sandwiches are great for parties, picnics, or as a fun lunch option.

Sweet Potato Fries

Ingredients:

- 2 large sweet potatoes
- 2 tablespoons olive oil
- 1 teaspoon paprika
- 1/2 teaspoon garlic powder
- 1/2 teaspoon onion powder
- 1/2 teaspoon ground cumin
- Salt and pepper to taste
- Optional: 1/4 teaspoon cayenne pepper (for a bit of heat)
- Optional: Fresh parsley or cilantro, chopped (for garnish)

Instructions:

1. **Preheat Oven:** Preheat your oven to 425°F (220°C). Line a baking sheet with parchment paper or lightly grease it with non-stick spray.
2. **Prepare Sweet Potatoes:** Peel the sweet potatoes and cut them into even-sized sticks or wedges. Aim for about 1/4 to 1/2 inch thick to ensure they cook evenly and become crispy.
3. **Season Fries:** In a large bowl, toss the sweet potato sticks with olive oil, paprika, garlic powder, onion powder, ground cumin, salt, and pepper. If you like a bit of heat, add cayenne pepper as well. Toss until the sweet potatoes are evenly coated with the oil and seasonings.
4. **Arrange on Baking Sheet:** Spread the seasoned sweet potato fries in a single layer on the prepared baking sheet. Make sure they are not overcrowded; this helps them get crispy.
5. **Bake:** Bake in the preheated oven for 20-25 minutes, flipping halfway through, until the fries are golden brown and crispy on the edges. The exact time may vary depending on the thickness of the fries and your oven.
6. **Serve:** Remove from the oven and let the fries cool slightly before serving. Garnish with fresh parsley or cilantro if desired. Serve warm with your favorite dipping sauce.

Tips:

- For extra crispiness, you can soak the cut sweet potatoes in water for 30 minutes before baking. Drain and pat dry thoroughly before tossing with oil and seasonings.
- To make these fries even healthier, consider using an air fryer if you have one. Cook at 400°F (200°C) for about 15 minutes, shaking the basket halfway through.
- Sweet potato fries can be seasoned with a variety of spices to suit your taste. Try adding cinnamon and a touch of brown sugar for a sweet twist, or rosemary and thyme for a more savory flavor.

Broccoli and Cheese Stuffed Potatoes

Ingredients:

- 4 large russet potatoes
- 1 cup broccoli florets (fresh or frozen)
- 1 cup shredded cheese (cheddar, Monterey Jack, or your choice)
- 1/2 cup milk
- 2 tablespoons butter
- 1/4 cup sour cream or Greek yogurt
- 1/4 cup grated Parmesan cheese
- 2 cloves garlic, minced
- Salt and pepper to taste
- Optional: 1/4 teaspoon crushed red pepper flakes (for a bit of heat)
- Optional: Chopped green onions or fresh parsley (for garnish)

Instructions:

1. **Preheat Oven:** Preheat your oven to 400°F (200°C).
2. **Bake Potatoes:** Wash and dry the russet potatoes. Pierce each potato with a fork several times. Place them directly on the oven rack or on a baking sheet. Bake for 45-60 minutes, or until tender when pierced with a fork. Remove from the oven and let cool slightly.
3. **Prepare Broccoli:** While the potatoes are baking, steam or microwave the broccoli florets until tender. If using frozen broccoli, cook according to package instructions. Chop the broccoli into small pieces.
4. **Prepare Potato Filling:** Once the potatoes are cool enough to handle, cut each potato in half lengthwise. Scoop out the flesh into a bowl, leaving a small border of potato around the edges to create a shell.
5. **Mash Potato Filling:** Add the butter, milk, and sour cream (or Greek yogurt) to the bowl with the scooped-out potato. Mash until smooth and creamy. Stir in the shredded cheese, grated Parmesan, minced garlic, and chopped broccoli. Season with salt, pepper, and crushed red pepper flakes if using.
6. **Stuff Potatoes:** Spoon the broccoli and cheese mixture back into the potato skins, mounding it up slightly.
7. **Bake Again:** Place the stuffed potatoes back on a baking sheet and bake for an additional 15-20 minutes, or until the tops are golden and the filling is heated through.
8. **Serve:** Garnish with chopped green onions or fresh parsley if desired. Serve warm.

Tips:

- You can use different types of cheese for varied flavors or a blend of cheeses for extra richness.
- For a bit of crunch, sprinkle some additional grated cheese on top of the stuffed potatoes before the final bake.

- These stuffed potatoes can be made ahead of time and reheated in the oven. Just cover them with foil to prevent drying out.

Corn and Black Bean Salad

Ingredients:

- 1 can (15 oz) black beans, drained and rinsed
- 1 cup corn kernels (fresh, frozen, or canned; if using frozen, thaw before using)
- 1 red bell pepper, diced
- 1/2 red onion, finely chopped
- 1/2 cup cherry or grape tomatoes, halved
- 1/4 cup chopped fresh cilantro (optional)
- 1 avocado, diced (optional, add just before serving to prevent browning)

For the Dressing:

- 3 tablespoons olive oil
- 2 tablespoons lime juice (about 1 lime)
- 1 tablespoon honey or maple syrup
- 1 teaspoon ground cumin
- 1/2 teaspoon chili powder (optional, for a bit of spice)
- Salt and pepper to taste

Instructions:

1. **Prepare Vegetables:** In a large bowl, combine the black beans, corn, red bell pepper, red onion, and cherry or grape tomatoes. If using, add the chopped cilantro.
2. **Make Dressing:** In a small bowl or jar, whisk together the olive oil, lime juice, honey (or maple syrup), ground cumin, and chili powder (if using). Season with salt and pepper to taste.
3. **Combine:** Pour the dressing over the salad and toss gently to combine, ensuring that all the ingredients are evenly coated.
4. **Add Avocado:** If adding avocado, gently fold it into the salad just before serving to prevent it from becoming mushy.
5. **Chill and Serve:** Refrigerate the salad for at least 30 minutes to allow the flavors to meld. Serve chilled or at room temperature.

Tips:

- For extra flavor, consider adding a pinch of cayenne pepper or a few dashes of hot sauce to the dressing.
- This salad can be customized with other ingredients such as chopped cucumber, diced jalapeño for heat, or crumbled feta cheese.
- It's a great addition to summer barbecues, picnics, or as a side dish for tacos or grilled meats.

Mini Sliders

Ingredients:

For the Patties:

- 1 pound ground beef (80% lean is ideal)
- 1/4 cup finely chopped onion
- 1 tablespoon Worcestershire sauce
- 1 teaspoon garlic powder
- 1/2 teaspoon paprika
- Salt and pepper to taste
- 12 mini slider buns

For the Toppings:

- 12 slices of cheese (American, cheddar, or your choice)
- Lettuce leaves
- Tomato slices
- Pickles
- Ketchup and mustard
- Mayonnaise

Instructions:

1. **Prepare Patties:** In a bowl, combine the ground beef, chopped onion, Worcestershire sauce, garlic powder, paprika, salt, and pepper. Mix until just combined; avoid overmixing to keep the patties tender.
2. **Form Patties:** Divide the mixture into 12 equal portions and shape each portion into a small patty, about 1/2 inch thick.
3. **Cook Patties:**
   - **Grilling:** Preheat the grill to medium-high heat. Grill the patties for 2-3 minutes per side, or until they reach an internal temperature of 160°F (71°C). Add a slice of cheese to each patty during the last minute of cooking to melt.
   - **Pan-Frying:** Heat a skillet over medium-high heat. Cook the patties for 2-3 minutes per side, or until they reach the desired level of doneness. Add cheese during the last minute of cooking.
4. **Toast Buns:** While the patties are cooking, slice the mini buns in half and toast them lightly on the grill or in a toaster for added texture.
5. **Assemble Sliders:** Spread condiments (ketchup, mustard, mayonnaise) on the bottom halves of the toasted buns. Place a patty on each bottom bun, then top with lettuce, tomato, pickles, and the top bun.
6. **Serve:** Arrange the mini sliders on a platter and serve immediately while they are still warm.

Tips:

- Customize the sliders with your favorite toppings or add extras like caramelized onions, sautéed mushrooms, or avocado slices.
- For a different flavor, try seasoning the patties with different spices or herbs, or using ground turkey or chicken instead of beef.
- If making sliders ahead of time, keep the patties and buns separate and assemble them just before serving to keep everything fresh.

Caprese Skewers

Ingredients:

- 1 pint cherry or grape tomatoes
- 8 ounces fresh mozzarella balls (bocconcini or ciliegine), drained
- Fresh basil leaves
- 2 tablespoons extra virgin olive oil
- 1 tablespoon balsamic glaze or reduction
- Salt and freshly ground black pepper to taste
- Wooden skewers or toothpicks

Instructions:

1. **Assemble Skewers:**
    - Thread a cherry tomato onto a skewer or toothpick.
    - Follow with a mozzarella ball.
    - Add a fresh basil leaf.
    - Repeat the process to fill the skewer or toothpick, usually 3-4 items per skewer, depending on size.
2. **Season:** Arrange the assembled skewers on a serving platter. Drizzle with extra virgin olive oil and balsamic glaze or reduction.
3. **Add Seasoning:** Season with salt and freshly ground black pepper to taste.
4. **Serve:** Serve immediately or chill until ready to serve. If preparing ahead of time, keep the skewers covered and refrigerated, and add the olive oil and balsamic glaze just before serving.

Tips:

- For added flavor, you can sprinkle some dried Italian herbs or freshly chopped basil over the skewers.
- If you can't find balsamic glaze, you can make your own by reducing balsamic vinegar in a saucepan until it thickens.
- These skewers are versatile and can be served as part of a larger appetizer spread or as a fresh, light addition to any meal.

Loaded Baked Potato Bites

Ingredients:

- 4 large russet potatoes
- 2 tablespoons olive oil
- 1 cup shredded cheddar cheese
- 1/2 cup cooked bacon, crumbled (about 4 strips)
- 1/4 cup sour cream or Greek yogurt
- 2 tablespoons chopped green onions or chives
- Salt and pepper to taste
- Optional: 1/4 cup grated Parmesan cheese
- Optional: Fresh parsley for garnish

Instructions:

1. **Preheat Oven:** Preheat your oven to 400°F (200°C). Line a baking sheet with parchment paper or lightly grease it with non-stick spray.
2. **Prepare Potatoes:** Wash and dry the russet potatoes. Cut them into bite-sized cubes, about 1/2 inch in size. Toss the potato cubes with olive oil, salt, and pepper.
3. **Bake Potatoes:** Spread the potato cubes in a single layer on the prepared baking sheet. Bake for 20-25 minutes, or until the potatoes are tender and golden brown, stirring halfway through for even cooking.
4. **Assemble Bites:** Remove the potatoes from the oven. Transfer the baked potato cubes to a large bowl. Sprinkle with shredded cheddar cheese and crumbled bacon. Return to the oven and bake for an additional 5-7 minutes, or until the cheese is melted and bubbly.
5. **Add Toppings:** Remove from the oven and drizzle with sour cream or Greek yogurt. Sprinkle with chopped green onions or chives. If desired, add grated Parmesan cheese and return to the oven for another minute or two to melt the cheese.
6. **Garnish and Serve:** Garnish with fresh parsley if desired. Serve warm.

Tips:

- For extra flavor, you can season the potato cubes with additional spices like paprika, garlic powder, or onion powder before baking.
- To make these bites ahead of time, bake the potatoes and assemble the toppings, then reheat them in the oven before serving.
- For a vegetarian version, omit the bacon or substitute with a plant-based alternative. You can also add other toppings like diced tomatoes, black olives, or jalapeños.

Roasted Chickpeas

Ingredients:

- 1 can (15 oz) chickpeas (garbanzo beans), drained and rinsed
- 1-2 tablespoons olive oil
- 1 teaspoon smoked paprika
- 1/2 teaspoon garlic powder
- 1/2 teaspoon onion powder
- 1/2 teaspoon ground cumin
- 1/4 teaspoon ground turmeric (optional)
- Salt to taste
- Optional: 1/4 teaspoon cayenne pepper or red pepper flakes (for heat)

Instructions:

1. **Preheat Oven:** Preheat your oven to 400°F (200°C). Line a baking sheet with parchment paper or lightly grease it.
2. **Prepare Chickpeas:** Pat the chickpeas dry with paper towels. This helps them become crispy during roasting.
3. **Season Chickpeas:** In a bowl, toss the chickpeas with olive oil, smoked paprika, garlic powder, onion powder, ground cumin, ground turmeric (if using), and salt. Add cayenne pepper or red pepper flakes if you like a bit of spice.
4. **Roast Chickpeas:** Spread the seasoned chickpeas in a single layer on the prepared baking sheet. Roast in the preheated oven for 20-30 minutes, shaking the pan or stirring the chickpeas halfway through to ensure even cooking. They should be golden brown and crispy.
5. **Cool and Serve:** Allow the roasted chickpeas to cool completely before serving. They will continue to crisp up as they cool.

Tips:

- Store leftover roasted chickpeas in an airtight container at room temperature for up to a week. They are best eaten within a few days for maximum crunch.
- Experiment with different seasonings to match your flavor preferences. For example, try adding curry powder, cinnamon and sugar, or your favorite spice blend.
- If you prefer a more intense flavor, try marinating the chickpeas in spices and olive oil before roasting. Just be sure to dry them thoroughly after marinating.

Sweet and Savory Rice Balls

Ingredients:

For the Rice Balls:

- 2 cups cooked rice (preferably short-grain or sushi rice, but any rice will work)
- 1 cup shredded cheese (cheddar, mozzarella, or your choice)
- 1/2 cup cooked bacon or ham, finely chopped (optional)
- 1/4 cup finely chopped green onions or chives
- 1/4 cup soy sauce
- 1 tablespoon olive oil
- 1 tablespoon sesame seeds (optional)
- Salt and pepper to taste

For the Sweet Coating (optional):

- 1/4 cup honey or maple syrup
- 1/4 teaspoon ground cinnamon
- 1 tablespoon sesame seeds or chopped nuts (optional)

Instructions:

1. **Prepare Rice:** If you don't already have cooked rice, prepare it according to package instructions. Let the rice cool slightly before using.
2. **Mix Ingredients:** In a large bowl, combine the cooked rice, shredded cheese, chopped bacon or ham (if using), green onions or chives, and soy sauce. Mix until well combined.
3. **Form Rice Balls:** Wet your hands slightly to prevent sticking. Take a small portion of the rice mixture and form it into a ball, about 1-2 inches in diameter. Place each rice ball on a plate.
4. **Add Coating (Optional):** If you'd like to add a sweet coating, mix the honey or maple syrup with ground cinnamon. Drizzle or brush the mixture over the rice balls. Sprinkle with sesame seeds or chopped nuts if desired.
5. **Cook Rice Balls:**
    - **Pan-Frying:** Heat olive oil in a skillet over medium heat. Add the rice balls and cook, turning occasionally, until they are golden brown and crispy on the outside, about 5-7 minutes.
    - **Baking (Healthier Option):** Preheat your oven to 375°F (190°C). Place the rice balls on a baking sheet lined with parchment paper. Bake for 15-20 minutes, or until golden and crispy.
6. **Serve:** Serve warm. You can enjoy these rice balls as a snack or as part of a meal.

Tips:

- For a variation, try adding vegetables like peas, corn, or diced bell peppers to the rice mixture.

- To make the rice balls extra crispy, you can roll them in panko breadcrumbs before cooking.
- If making ahead of time, store the rice balls in an airtight container in the refrigerator. Reheat in the oven or skillet to maintain crispiness.

Ham and Pineapple Skewers

Ingredients:

- 1 pound ham, cut into bite-sized cubes (use pre-cooked or leftover ham)
- 1 can (20 oz) pineapple chunks, drained (or use fresh pineapple cut into chunks)
- 1 red bell pepper, cut into bite-sized pieces
- 1 green bell pepper, cut into bite-sized pieces
- 1 small red onion, cut into bite-sized pieces
- 2 tablespoons olive oil
- 2 tablespoons honey
- 1 tablespoon soy sauce
- 1 teaspoon garlic powder
- 1 teaspoon ground ginger (optional)
- Salt and pepper to taste
- Wooden skewers, soaked in water for 30 minutes to prevent burning

Instructions:

1. **Prepare Ingredients:** If using fresh pineapple, cut it into chunks. Cut the ham, bell peppers, and onion into similar-sized pieces for even cooking.
2. **Make Marinade:** In a small bowl, whisk together olive oil, honey, soy sauce, garlic powder, ground ginger (if using), salt, and pepper.
3. **Marinate Ingredients:** In a large bowl, toss the ham, pineapple chunks, bell peppers, and onion with the marinade. Let it sit for about 15-20 minutes to absorb the flavors.
4. **Assemble Skewers:** Thread the marinated ham, pineapple chunks, bell peppers, and onion onto the soaked skewers, alternating the ingredients.
5. **Cook Skewers:**
    - **Grilling:** Preheat your grill to medium-high heat. Grill the skewers for 2-3 minutes per side, or until the ham is heated through and the vegetables are slightly charred.
    - **Oven Broiling:** Preheat your broiler. Place the skewers on a baking sheet lined with foil. Broil for 2-3 minutes per side, or until the ham is heated through and the vegetables are slightly charred.
    - **Pan-Frying:** Heat a skillet over medium heat. Cook the skewers, turning occasionally, for about 6-8 minutes or until heated through and slightly caramelized.
6. **Serve:** Remove from heat and serve immediately. These skewers can be served with a side of dipping sauce or over rice.

Tips:

- For added flavor, sprinkle the skewers with chopped fresh herbs like cilantro or parsley before serving.

- If you prefer a bit of spice, add a pinch of red pepper flakes or a splash of hot sauce to the marinade.
- You can also use other vegetables such as zucchini or cherry tomatoes to customize the skewers to your taste.

Pasta and Veggie Soup

Ingredients:

- 1 tablespoon olive oil
- 1 medium onion, diced
- 2 cloves garlic, minced
- 2 medium carrots, sliced
- 2 celery stalks, sliced
- 1 red bell pepper, diced
- 1 zucchini, diced
- 1 cup green beans, chopped (fresh or frozen)
- 1 can (14.5 oz) diced tomatoes (with juices)
- 4 cups vegetable broth (or chicken broth)
- 1 cup small pasta (e.g., elbow macaroni, ditalini, or small shells)
- 1 teaspoon dried basil
- 1 teaspoon dried oregano
- 1/2 teaspoon dried thyme
- Salt and pepper to taste
- 1 cup spinach or kale, chopped (optional)
- 1/2 cup grated Parmesan cheese (optional, for serving)
- Fresh parsley or basil, chopped (for garnish, optional)

Instructions:

1. **Sauté Vegetables:** Heat the olive oil in a large pot over medium heat. Add the diced onion and garlic, and sauté until the onion is translucent, about 3-4 minutes.
2. **Add Vegetables:** Add the sliced carrots, celery, red bell pepper, zucchini, and green beans. Cook for another 5-7 minutes, until the vegetables begin to soften.
3. **Add Tomatoes and Broth:** Stir in the diced tomatoes with their juices and the vegetable broth. Bring to a boil.
4. **Simmer:** Reduce the heat to low and add the dried basil, oregano, thyme, salt, and pepper. Simmer for about 10 minutes, until the vegetables are tender.
5. **Cook Pasta:** Add the pasta to the soup and cook according to the pasta package instructions, usually 8-10 minutes, or until al dente. Stir occasionally to prevent the pasta from sticking.
6. **Add Greens:** If using, stir in the chopped spinach or kale and cook for an additional 2-3 minutes until wilted.
7. **Adjust Seasoning:** Taste and adjust the seasoning with additional salt and pepper if needed.
8. **Serve:** Ladle the soup into bowls and sprinkle with grated Parmesan cheese and fresh parsley or basil if desired. Serve hot.

Tips:

- You can use any vegetables you have on hand or prefer. For a heartier soup, add potatoes or sweet potatoes.
- For a protein boost, add cooked chicken, turkey, or beans to the soup.
- Store leftovers in an airtight container in the refrigerator for up to 3-4 days. The soup may thicken as it sits, so you can add a little water or broth when reheating if needed.
- If you're making the soup ahead of time, cook the pasta separately and add it to the soup just before serving to prevent it from becoming too mushy.

Chicken Caesar Wraps

Ingredients:

- 2 cups cooked chicken breast, sliced or shredded (grilled, baked, or rotisserie)
- 4 large flour tortillas or wraps
- 1 cup Romaine lettuce, chopped
- 1/2 cup grated Parmesan cheese
- 1/4 cup Caesar dressing (store-bought or homemade)
- 1/4 teaspoon garlic powder (optional)
- 1/4 teaspoon black pepper
- Optional: Croutons for extra crunch

Instructions:

1. **Prepare Chicken:** If you haven't already, cook and slice or shred the chicken breast. You can season it with salt and pepper, or use leftover cooked chicken.
2. **Mix Dressing:** In a large bowl, combine the chopped Romaine lettuce with Caesar dressing. Toss until the lettuce is evenly coated.
3. **Assemble Wraps:** Lay a tortilla flat on a clean surface. Evenly distribute the dressed lettuce in the center of the tortilla.
4. **Add Chicken and Cheese:** Top the lettuce with the sliced or shredded chicken and sprinkle with grated Parmesan cheese. If using, add croutons for extra crunch.
5. **Season:** Sprinkle garlic powder and black pepper over the chicken if desired.
6. **Wrap and Serve:** Fold the sides of the tortilla inward, then roll it up from the bottom to enclose the filling. Slice in half if desired.
7. **Serve:** Serve immediately, or wrap in foil or parchment paper for an on-the-go meal.

Tips:

- For a homemade Caesar dressing, blend together mayonnaise, lemon juice, Dijon mustard, minced garlic, Worcestershire sauce, grated Parmesan cheese, salt, and pepper.
- You can add additional ingredients such as sliced cherry tomatoes, avocado, or bacon bits for more flavor.
- If you prefer a warm wrap, you can toast it in a skillet over medium heat until golden and crispy on the outside.
- These wraps can be made ahead of time and stored in the refrigerator for a few hours. For best results, add the dressing just before serving to prevent the wraps from becoming soggy.

Tuna Melt Sandwiches

Ingredients:

- 1 can (5 oz) tuna, drained
- 2 tablespoons mayonnaise
- 1 tablespoon Dijon mustard
- 1/4 cup finely chopped celery
- 1/4 cup finely chopped onion
- 1 tablespoon lemon juice
- Salt and pepper to taste
- 4 slices of bread (white, whole wheat, or your choice)
- 4 slices of cheese (cheddar, Swiss, or American)
- 2 tablespoons butter (for spreading on the bread)
- Optional: Tomato slices or pickles for added flavor

Instructions:

1. **Prepare Tuna Salad:**
    - In a bowl, mix together the drained tuna, mayonnaise, Dijon mustard, chopped celery, chopped onion, and lemon juice. Season with salt and pepper to taste. Stir until well combined.
2. **Prepare Bread:**
    - Spread butter on one side of each slice of bread. This will be the side that gets toasted.
3. **Assemble Sandwiches:**
    - Heat a skillet over medium heat. Place two slices of bread, buttered side down, in the skillet.
    - Spoon a generous amount of the tuna salad onto each slice of bread in the skillet. Top with a slice of cheese.
    - Place the remaining slices of bread on top, buttered side up.
4. **Cook Sandwiches:**
    - Cook the sandwiches for 3-4 minutes on each side, or until the bread is golden brown and crispy and the cheese is melted. You can press down slightly with a spatula to ensure even toasting and melting.
5. **Serve:**
    - Remove the sandwiches from the skillet and let them cool for a minute before slicing in half. Serve warm.

Tips:

- For extra flavor, you can add tomato slices, pickles, or even a slice of bacon to the sandwich before grilling.
- You can use any type of bread or cheese you prefer. Rye bread or sourdough can add a nice twist.

- If you like a bit of spice, add a dash of hot sauce or a pinch of red pepper flakes to the tuna salad.
- To make these sandwiches ahead of time, prepare the tuna salad and keep it in the refrigerator. Assemble and grill the sandwiches just before serving.

Veggie Sushi Rolls

Ingredients:

- 2 cups sushi rice (short-grain rice)
- 2 1/2 cups water
- 1/2 cup rice vinegar
- 2 tablespoons sugar
- 1 teaspoon salt
- 4-5 sheets nori (seaweed)
- 1 cucumber, peeled and cut into thin strips
- 1 avocado, sliced
- 1 medium carrot, peeled and cut into thin strips
- 1/2 bell pepper (any color), sliced into thin strips
- Optional: 1/4 cup cream cheese, thinly spread (for added creaminess)
- Soy sauce, for dipping
- Pickled ginger, for serving
- Wasabi, for serving

Instructions:

1. **Prepare Sushi Rice:**
    - Rinse the sushi rice under cold water until the water runs clear. This removes excess starch.
    - Combine the rinsed rice and water in a rice cooker or a medium saucepan. Cook according to the rice cooker's instructions or bring to a boil, then reduce heat, cover, and simmer for 20 minutes. Remove from heat and let it sit, covered, for 10 minutes.
    - In a small bowl, mix the rice vinegar, sugar, and salt until dissolved. Gently fold the vinegar mixture into the cooked rice. Let the rice cool to room temperature.
2. **Prepare Vegetables:**
    - Prepare and slice the vegetables into thin, matchstick-sized strips.
3. **Assemble Sushi Rolls:**
    - Place a bamboo sushi mat on a clean surface and cover it with plastic wrap. Place a sheet of nori, shiny side down, on the mat.
    - Wet your hands with water to prevent sticking, and spread a thin, even layer of sushi rice over the nori, leaving about 1 inch at the top edge of the nori sheet. Press the rice down gently but firmly.
    - Arrange the sliced vegetables (and cream cheese if using) in a line across the rice, about 1 inch from the bottom edge of the nori.
4. **Roll Sushi:**
    - Using the bamboo mat, carefully lift the edge of the nori closest to you and start rolling it tightly over the filling. Use gentle pressure to make a firm roll. Once you reach the exposed edge of the nori, seal the roll by pressing it down lightly.
    - Repeat with the remaining nori sheets and filling ingredients.

5. **Slice Rolls:**
   - Using a sharp knife, slice each roll into bite-sized pieces. To prevent sticking, you can dip the knife in water between cuts.
6. **Serve:**
   - Arrange the sushi rolls on a platter. Serve with soy sauce, pickled ginger, and wasabi.

Tips:

- If you don't have a bamboo sushi mat, you can use a clean kitchen towel to help roll the sushi.
- Feel free to customize the fillings based on your preferences, such as adding thinly sliced bell peppers, radishes, or fresh herbs.
- For a bit of extra flavor, lightly toast the nori sheets before using them.

Enjoy your homemade veggie sushi rolls!

Breakfast Burritos

Ingredients:

- 6 large flour tortillas
- 6 large eggs
- 1/4 cup milk
- 1 tablespoon butter or oil
- 1 cup shredded cheddar cheese
- 1 cup cooked and crumbled breakfast sausage or bacon (optional)
- 1 cup cooked and diced potatoes (e.g., hash browns or roasted potatoes)
- 1/2 cup diced bell peppers (any color)
- 1/2 cup diced onions
- 1/2 cup salsa or diced tomatoes (optional)
- Salt and pepper to taste
- Fresh cilantro or green onions for garnish (optional)

Instructions:

1. **Prepare Fillings:**
    - **Potatoes:** If not using pre-cooked potatoes, dice and cook them until tender and lightly browned. You can use leftover roasted potatoes or cook some hash browns.
    - **Veggies:** In a skillet, sauté diced onions and bell peppers until softened. Set aside.
2. **Scramble Eggs:**
    - In a bowl, whisk together the eggs, milk, salt, and pepper.
    - Heat butter or oil in a large skillet over medium heat. Pour in the egg mixture and cook, stirring occasionally, until the eggs are scrambled and cooked through. Remove from heat.
3. **Assemble Burritos:**
    - Warm the flour tortillas in a dry skillet or microwave for a few seconds until pliable.
    - Lay a tortilla flat on a clean surface. Spoon some scrambled eggs down the center of the tortilla.
    - Add some cooked potatoes, crumbled sausage or bacon (if using), sautéed veggies, and shredded cheese.
    - If desired, add a spoonful of salsa or diced tomatoes.
4. **Roll Burritos:**
    - Fold the sides of the tortilla inward over the filling, then roll up from the bottom to enclose the filling tightly.
5. **Cook Burritos (Optional):**
    - For a crispy exterior, heat a skillet over medium heat. Place the burritos seam-side down in the skillet and cook until golden brown, about 2-3 minutes per side.
6. **Serve:**
    - Serve warm, garnished with fresh cilantro or green onions if desired. You can also serve with extra salsa, hot sauce, or avocado slices on the side.

Tips:

- To make these burritos ahead of time, assemble and wrap them tightly in foil or plastic wrap. Store in the refrigerator for up to 3 days or freeze for up to 2 months. To reheat, microwave until heated through or bake from frozen at 375°F (190°C) for 20-25 minutes.
- Customize your burritos with other fillings like sautéed mushrooms, spinach, or different types of cheese.
- If you prefer a spicier kick, add chopped jalapeños or a sprinkle of chili powder to the filling.

Turkey and Veggie Muffins

Ingredients:

- 1 cup cooked turkey breast, diced (or ground turkey)
- 1 cup finely chopped vegetables (e.g., bell peppers, carrots, spinach, or zucchini)

- 1/2 cup grated cheese (cheddar, mozzarella, or your choice)
- 4 large eggs
- 1/2 cup milk (or any plant-based milk)
- 1/2 cup whole wheat flour (or all-purpose flour)
- 1/2 teaspoon baking powder
- 1/4 teaspoon salt
- 1/4 teaspoon black pepper
- 1/4 teaspoon garlic powder (optional)
- 1/4 teaspoon dried oregano or basil (optional)
- Cooking spray or a little oil for greasing the muffin tin

Instructions:

1. **Preheat Oven:** Preheat your oven to 375°F (190°C). Grease a muffin tin with cooking spray or lightly brush with oil, or use paper liners.
2. **Prepare Ingredients:** If using ground turkey, cook it in a skillet over medium heat until fully cooked. If using cooked turkey breast, dice it into small pieces.
3. **Mix Wet Ingredients:** In a large bowl, whisk together the eggs and milk until well combined.
4. **Combine Dry Ingredients:** In a separate bowl, mix the flour, baking powder, salt, pepper, garlic powder, and dried herbs (if using).
5. **Combine Ingredients:** Add the turkey, chopped vegetables, and cheese to the wet ingredients. Stir to combine.
6. **Add Dry Ingredients:** Gradually add the dry ingredients to the wet mixture, stirring until just combined. The mixture should be somewhat thick.
7. **Fill Muffin Tin:** Spoon the batter evenly into the prepared muffin tin, filling each cup about 3/4 full.
8. **Bake:** Bake in the preheated oven for 20-25 minutes, or until the muffins are golden brown and a toothpick inserted into the center comes out clean.
9. **Cool:** Allow the muffins to cool in the tin for a few minutes before transferring them to a wire rack to cool completely.
10. **Serve:** Serve warm or at room temperature. These muffins can be enjoyed on their own or with a side of fruit or yogurt.

Tips:

- For added flavor and nutrition, consider adding finely chopped herbs like parsley or cilantro to the mixture.
- You can customize the muffins with different vegetables and cheese based on what you have on hand.
- To freeze, let the muffins cool completely, then store them in a freezer-safe bag or container. Reheat in the microwave or oven before serving.

Cheesy Cauliflower Bites

Ingredients:

- 1 medium head of cauliflower, cut into bite-sized florets
- 1 cup shredded cheddar cheese (or your favorite cheese)

- 1/2 cup grated Parmesan cheese
- 1/2 cup breadcrumbs (Panko or regular)
- 2 large eggs
- 1/2 cup milk (or any plant-based milk)
- 1 teaspoon garlic powder
- 1 teaspoon onion powder
- 1/2 teaspoon dried oregano or basil (optional)
- Salt and pepper to taste
- Cooking spray or a little oil for greasing

Instructions:

1. **Preheat Oven:** Preheat your oven to 400°F (200°C). Line a baking sheet with parchment paper or lightly grease it.
2. **Prepare Cauliflower:** Wash and cut the cauliflower into bite-sized florets.
3. **Make Breading Mixture:**
   - In a bowl, combine the breadcrumbs, shredded cheddar cheese, grated Parmesan cheese, garlic powder, onion powder, dried oregano or basil (if using), salt, and pepper.
4. **Prepare Dipping Station:**
   - In a separate bowl, whisk together the eggs and milk.
   - Dip each cauliflower floret into the egg mixture, allowing any excess to drip off, then coat it in the breadcrumb mixture. Press gently to help the coating stick.
5. **Arrange Cauliflower:**
   - Place the coated cauliflower florets on the prepared baking sheet in a single layer.
6. **Bake:**
   - Bake in the preheated oven for 20-25 minutes, or until the cauliflower is tender and the coating is golden brown and crispy. Flip the bites halfway through cooking for even browning.
7. **Serve:**
   - Remove from the oven and let cool for a few minutes before serving. Serve warm with a side of marinara sauce, ranch dressing, or your favorite dipping sauce.

Tips:

- For a spicier kick, add a pinch of red pepper flakes to the breadcrumb mixture.
- You can use other types of cheese or add a mix of cheeses for varied flavor.
- If you prefer a lower-carb option, you can use almond flour or crushed pork rinds instead of breadcrumbs.
- To make these bites ahead of time, bake and cool them, then store in an airtight container in the refrigerator. Reheat in the oven to restore crispiness.

Fruit Smoothie Bowls

Ingredients:

For the Smoothie Base:

- 1 cup frozen berries (such as strawberries, blueberries, or raspberries)
- 1 banana (fresh or frozen)
- 1/2 cup Greek yogurt (plain or vanilla)
- 1/2 cup milk (or any plant-based milk)
- 1 tablespoon honey or maple syrup (optional, for added sweetness)
- 1 tablespoon chia seeds or flaxseeds (optional, for extra nutrition)

Toppings:

- Fresh fruit (e.g., sliced banana, berries, kiwi, mango)
- Granola
- Nuts or seeds (e.g., almonds, walnuts, chia seeds)
- Coconut flakes
- Honey or maple syrup
- Fresh mint leaves (optional)

Instructions:

1. **Prepare Smoothie Base:**
    - In a blender, combine the frozen berries, banana, Greek yogurt, milk, honey or maple syrup (if using), and chia seeds or flaxseeds (if using).
    - Blend until smooth and creamy. If the mixture is too thick, you can add a little more milk to reach your desired consistency.
2. **Pour into Bowls:**
    - Divide the smoothie mixture evenly between bowls.
3. **Add Toppings:**
    - Arrange your choice of toppings on top of the smoothie base. Get creative with the arrangement to make it visually appealing. You can add fresh fruit slices, granola, nuts, seeds, coconut flakes, and a drizzle of honey or maple syrup.
4. **Serve:**
    - Serve immediately for the best texture and flavor. Enjoy with a spoon!

Tips:

- Feel free to use any combination of fruits you like. For a tropical twist, use pineapple or mango. For a more indulgent flavor, add a spoonful of cocoa powder or peanut butter to the smoothie base.
- If you prefer a thicker texture, you can freeze the fruit beforehand or reduce the amount of milk.
- For an added protein boost, use protein yogurt or add a scoop of protein powder to the smoothie base.
- You can make the smoothie base ahead of time and store it in the freezer. Just let it thaw slightly before adding toppings and serving.

Chicken and Rice Casserole

Ingredients:

- 2 cups cooked chicken, shredded or diced (use rotisserie chicken or cook your own)
- 1 cup uncooked long-grain white rice

- 2 cups chicken broth
- 1 cup milk (or any plant-based milk)
- 1 can (10.5 oz) cream of chicken soup (or homemade equivalent)
- 1 cup frozen peas and carrots (or fresh if preferred)
- 1 small onion, finely chopped
- 2 cloves garlic, minced
- 1 cup shredded cheddar cheese (or your favorite cheese)
- 1/2 teaspoon dried thyme (optional)
- 1/2 teaspoon dried rosemary (optional)
- 1/2 teaspoon paprika
- Salt and pepper to taste
- 1 tablespoon olive oil or butter (for sautéing)
- 1/2 cup breadcrumbs (optional, for topping)
- 2 tablespoons melted butter (optional, for topping)

Instructions:

1. **Preheat Oven:** Preheat your oven to 375°F (190°C). Grease a 9x13-inch baking dish or similar-sized casserole dish.
2. **Cook Vegetables:**
   - In a skillet, heat the olive oil or butter over medium heat. Add the chopped onion and cook until translucent, about 3-4 minutes.
   - Add the minced garlic and cook for another 1 minute, until fragrant.
3. **Prepare Casserole Mixture:**
   - In a large mixing bowl, combine the cooked chicken, uncooked rice, chicken broth, milk, cream of chicken soup, frozen peas and carrots, sautéed onions and garlic, shredded cheese, dried thyme, dried rosemary, paprika, salt, and pepper. Stir well to combine.
4. **Assemble Casserole:**
   - Pour the mixture into the prepared baking dish and spread it evenly.
5. **Add Topping (Optional):**
   - If you like a crunchy topping, mix the breadcrumbs with melted butter and sprinkle evenly over the casserole.
6. **Bake:**
   - Bake in the preheated oven for 45-50 minutes, or until the rice is tender and the casserole is bubbly and golden on top. If using breadcrumbs, they should be golden brown and crispy.
7. **Cool and Serve:**
   - Allow the casserole to cool for a few minutes before serving. This helps it set and makes it easier to serve.

Tips:

- Feel free to substitute the cream of chicken soup with a homemade version or use a different cream soup like mushroom.

- For a lighter version, use reduced-fat cream of chicken soup and cheese.
- You can add other vegetables like bell peppers, mushrooms, or corn for more variety.
- If you prefer a spicier kick, add a pinch of cayenne pepper or a dash of hot sauce to the mixture.

This Chicken and Rice Casserole is a versatile and comforting dish that can be adapted to your taste preferences and is sure to be a hit with the whole family!

Mini Veggie Frittatas

Ingredients:

- 6 large eggs
- 1/4 cup milk (or any plant-based milk)

- 1 cup shredded cheese (cheddar, mozzarella, or your choice)
- 1 cup finely chopped vegetables (e.g., bell peppers, spinach, onions, mushrooms, zucchini)
- 1/4 cup chopped fresh herbs (optional, e.g., parsley, chives)
- Salt and pepper to taste
- 1 tablespoon olive oil or butter (for greasing the muffin tin)
- Optional: 1/2 cup cooked bacon, sausage, or ham, diced (for added protein)

Instructions:

1. **Preheat Oven:** Preheat your oven to 375°F (190°C). Grease a 12-cup muffin tin with olive oil or butter, or use paper liners.
2. **Prepare Vegetables:**
   - If using raw vegetables that need cooking (like mushrooms or bell peppers), sauté them in a skillet with a little olive oil until tender. Let them cool slightly before adding them to the egg mixture.
3. **Mix Egg Base:**
   - In a large bowl, whisk together the eggs, milk, salt, and pepper until well combined.
4. **Add Cheese and Veggies:**
   - Stir in the shredded cheese, cooked vegetables, fresh herbs (if using), and any additional protein like bacon or sausage.
5. **Fill Muffin Tin:**
   - Spoon the mixture evenly into the muffin tin cups, filling each cup about 3/4 full.
6. **Bake:**
   - Bake in the preheated oven for 20-25 minutes, or until the frittatas are puffed and golden brown, and a toothpick inserted into the center comes out clean.
7. **Cool and Serve:**
   - Let the mini frittatas cool in the tin for a few minutes before transferring them to a wire rack to cool completely.
8. **Serve:**
   - Serve warm, at room temperature, or store in the refrigerator for up to 4 days. These frittatas can also be frozen for up to 2 months. Reheat in the microwave or oven before serving.

Tips:

- Feel free to experiment with different combinations of vegetables and cheeses to suit your taste preferences.
- For a dairy-free version, use a plant-based milk and cheese alternative.
- Mini frittatas are perfect for meal prep. Make a batch at the beginning of the week and grab them for a quick breakfast or snack.

These Mini Veggie Frittatas are versatile and can be customized to include your favorite veggies and proteins, making them a great addition to your meal rotation!

Cheese-Stuffed Meatballs

Ingredients:

For the Meatballs:

- 1 pound ground beef (or a mix of beef and pork)
- 1/2 cup breadcrumbs (Panko or regular)
- 1/4 cup grated Parmesan cheese
- 1/4 cup chopped fresh parsley (or 2 tablespoons dried parsley)
- 1/4 cup finely chopped onion
- 2 cloves garlic, minced
- 1 large egg
- 1/4 cup milk
- Salt and pepper to taste
- 1 cup shredded mozzarella cheese (or any cheese that melts well)

For Cooking:

- 1 cup marinara sauce (store-bought or homemade)
- 1 tablespoon olive oil (if pan-frying)

Instructions:

1. **Preheat Oven (if baking):** Preheat your oven to 375°F (190°C). Line a baking sheet with parchment paper or lightly grease it.
2. **Prepare Meatball Mixture:**
   - In a large bowl, combine the ground beef, breadcrumbs, Parmesan cheese, parsley, onion, garlic, egg, milk, salt, and pepper. Mix until well combined, but don't overwork the meat.
3. **Shape Meatballs:**
   - Take a small amount of the meat mixture and flatten it in your hand. Place a small cube of mozzarella cheese in the center, then fold the meat around the cheese and roll it into a ball. Ensure the cheese is completely enclosed. Repeat with the remaining meat mixture.
4. **Cook Meatballs:**
   - **To Bake:** Place the meatballs on the prepared baking sheet. Bake in the preheated oven for 20-25 minutes, or until cooked through and browned on the outside.
   - **To Pan-Fry:** Heat olive oil in a skillet over medium heat. Add the meatballs and cook, turning occasionally, for 10-12 minutes, or until cooked through and browned on all sides.
5. **Heat Marinara Sauce:**
   - While the meatballs are cooking, heat the marinara sauce in a saucepan over medium heat.
6. **Serve:**
   - Once the meatballs are cooked, add them to the marinara sauce to coat. Serve with pasta, over a sub roll for a meatball sandwich, or alongside a salad or vegetables.

Tips:

- For an extra cheesy surprise, you can freeze the cheese cubes before using them. This helps the cheese stay inside the meatball during cooking.
- If you prefer a different cheese, feel free to use provolone, cheddar, or any cheese that melts well.
- These meatballs can also be made ahead of time and stored in the freezer. Reheat them in the microwave or oven, and add them to your favorite sauce.

Cheese-Stuffed Meatballs add a delicious twist to a classic favorite, making them a hit with kids and adults alike!

DIY Veggie Nachos

Ingredients:

For the Nachos:

- 1 bag (10-12 oz) tortilla chips
- 1 cup shredded cheese (cheddar, Monterey Jack, or a blend)

- 1 cup black beans, drained and rinsed
- 1 cup corn kernels (fresh, frozen, or canned)
- 1 bell pepper, diced
- 1 small onion, diced
- 1 cup cherry tomatoes, halved
- 1 cup sliced black olives (optional)
- 1/2 cup chopped fresh cilantro (optional)

For the Toppings:

- 1 avocado, sliced or diced
- 1/2 cup sour cream or Greek yogurt
- 1/2 cup salsa or pico de gallo
- 1/2 cup sliced jalapeños (fresh or pickled, optional)
- Lime wedges for serving

Instructions:

1. **Preheat Oven (if baking):** Preheat your oven to 400°F (200°C).
2. **Prepare Veggies:**
    - If using frozen corn, thaw and drain it. If using fresh corn, you can cook it briefly in a skillet or boil it until tender.
    - Dice the bell pepper and onion, and halve the cherry tomatoes.
3. **Layer Nachos:**
    - On a large baking sheet or oven-safe dish, spread a layer of tortilla chips.
    - Sprinkle half of the shredded cheese evenly over the chips.
    - Add black beans, corn, diced bell pepper, onion, and cherry tomatoes. Scatter some sliced black olives if using.
    - Top with the remaining shredded cheese.
4. **Bake:**
    - Bake in the preheated oven for 10-15 minutes, or until the cheese is melted and bubbly, and the veggies are heated through.
5. **Add Fresh Toppings:**
    - Once out of the oven, garnish with chopped fresh cilantro and any other fresh toppings you like, such as sliced avocado or additional jalapeños.
6. **Serve:**
    - Serve the nachos warm with sour cream or Greek yogurt, salsa or pico de gallo, and lime wedges on the side.

Tips:

- Feel free to customize the veggies based on what you have on hand or what you prefer. Zucchini, mushrooms, or spinach can also be great additions.
- For a protein boost, you can add grilled chicken, beef, or tofu.

- If you want to make these nachos ahead of time, prepare the veggie layer and cheese, then bake just before serving to ensure the chips stay crispy.
- To make them even healthier, use baked tortilla chips or make your own tortilla chips from whole grain tortillas.

Enjoy your DIY Veggie Nachos with all your favorite toppings!

Chicken and Spinach Pasta

Ingredients:

- 12 oz (340 g) pasta (penne, fusilli, or your choice)

- 2 tablespoons olive oil
- 1 pound (450 g) boneless, skinless chicken breasts or thighs, diced
- 1 small onion, finely chopped
- 3 cloves garlic, minced
- 1 cup cherry tomatoes, halved (or 1 can diced tomatoes, drained)
- 2 cups fresh spinach, washed and dried
- 1/2 cup chicken broth
- 1/4 cup heavy cream (or milk for a lighter version)
- 1/2 cup grated Parmesan cheese
- Salt and pepper to taste
- 1/2 teaspoon dried oregano or basil (optional)
- Fresh basil or parsley for garnish (optional)

Instructions:

1. **Cook Pasta:**
   - Bring a large pot of salted water to a boil. Cook the pasta according to the package instructions until al dente. Drain and set aside.
2. **Cook Chicken:**
   - In a large skillet or pan, heat olive oil over medium-high heat. Add the diced chicken and cook until browned and cooked through, about 5-7 minutes. Season with salt and pepper. Remove the chicken from the pan and set aside.
3. **Sauté Vegetables:**
   - In the same pan, add a little more olive oil if needed. Sauté the chopped onion until translucent, about 3-4 minutes.
   - Add the minced garlic and cook for an additional 1 minute until fragrant.
4. **Add Tomatoes:**
   - Stir in the cherry tomatoes (or canned diced tomatoes) and cook for 3-4 minutes until they start to soften.
5. **Combine Ingredients:**
   - Return the cooked chicken to the pan. Add the chicken broth and heavy cream. Stir to combine and let it simmer for 2-3 minutes.
6. **Add Spinach and Pasta:**
   - Stir in the fresh spinach and cook until wilted, about 1-2 minutes.
   - Add the cooked pasta to the skillet and toss everything together until well combined and heated through.
7. **Finish:**
   - Stir in the grated Parmesan cheese and adjust seasoning with salt, pepper, and dried oregano or basil, if using.
8. **Serve:**
   - Serve the pasta warm, garnished with fresh basil or parsley if desired.

Tips:

- You can add other vegetables like bell peppers, mushrooms, or zucchini for more variety.

- For a bit of heat, add a pinch of red pepper flakes to the skillet.
- If you prefer a lighter version, you can use half-and-half or a combination of milk and broth instead of heavy cream.
- Leftovers can be stored in an airtight container in the refrigerator for up to 3 days and reheated gently.

Enjoy your delicious and creamy Chicken and Spinach Pasta!

Mini Taco Bar

Ingredients:

For the Taco Fillings:

- **Ground Beef or Turkey:**
    - 1 pound (450 g) ground beef or ground turkey
    - 1 packet taco seasoning mix (or homemade seasoning)
    - 1/2 cup water (as per seasoning packet instructions)
- **Vegetarian Option:**
    - 1 can (15 oz) black beans, drained and rinsed
    - 1 cup corn kernels (fresh, frozen, or canned)
    - 1 teaspoon ground cumin
    - 1/2 teaspoon chili powder
    - 1/2 teaspoon garlic powder
    - Salt and pepper to taste

For the Taco Shells:

- **Hard Taco Shells:** Store-bought or homemade
- **Soft Tortillas:** Small flour or corn tortillas, warmed

Toppings:

- Shredded lettuce
- Diced tomatoes
- Sliced jalapeños
- Shredded cheese (cheddar, Monterey Jack, or a blend)
- Sour cream or Greek yogurt
- Salsa or pico de gallo
- Guacamole or sliced avocado
- Fresh cilantro, chopped
- Lime wedges
- Sliced red onions
- Sliced olives (optional)

Instructions:

1. **Prepare the Taco Fillings:**
    - **Ground Beef or Turkey:**
        1. In a skillet over medium heat, cook the ground beef or turkey until browned and cooked through, breaking it up with a spoon as it cooks.
        2. Drain any excess fat, if needed.
        3. Add the taco seasoning mix and water (according to the packet instructions). Simmer for 5 minutes until the sauce thickens and the flavors meld.
    - **Vegetarian Option:**
        1. In a skillet over medium heat, combine the black beans, corn, ground cumin, chili powder, garlic powder, salt, and pepper.

2. Cook until heated through and flavors are well combined, about 5 minutes.
2. **Prepare Taco Shells:**
    - If using hard taco shells, follow the package instructions to heat them in the oven.
    - For soft tortillas, warm them in a skillet over medium heat or in the microwave, covered with a damp paper towel.
3. **Set Up the Taco Bar:**
    - Arrange the taco shells and tortillas on a serving platter or in separate containers.
    - Place the prepared taco fillings in serving bowls.
    - Arrange the toppings in separate bowls or dishes, so guests can choose their favorites.
4. **Serve:**
    - Let everyone build their own tacos, starting with their choice of shell or tortilla and adding their preferred fillings and toppings.

Tips:

- To make the taco bar even more convenient, provide small serving spoons and tongs for each topping.
- For a more varied taco bar, consider adding additional protein options like grilled chicken, shrimp, or tofu.
- For a fun twist, include some unusual toppings like pickled radishes, crumbled feta cheese, or hot sauce varieties.

A Mini Taco Bar is not only delicious but also adds a fun, interactive element to your meal, making it a hit with guests of all ages!

Stuffed Bell Peppers

Ingredients:

- 4 large bell peppers (any color)
- 1 tablespoon olive oil
- 1 small onion, finely chopped
- 2 cloves garlic, minced
- 1 pound (450 g) ground beef, ground turkey, or plant-based ground meat
- 1 cup cooked rice (white, brown, or wild)
- 1 can (14.5 oz) diced tomatoes, drained
- 1/2 cup tomato sauce (or marinara sauce)
- 1 cup shredded cheese (cheddar, mozzarella, or a blend)
- 1 teaspoon dried oregano
- 1/2 teaspoon dried basil
- 1/2 teaspoon paprika
- Salt and pepper to taste
- Fresh parsley or basil for garnish (optional)

Instructions:

1. **Prepare Bell Peppers:**
    - Preheat your oven to 375°F (190°C).
    - Cut the tops off the bell peppers and remove the seeds and membranes. You can trim a small slice off the bottom of each pepper if they don't sit flat, but be careful not to cut through.
    - Lightly brush the outside of the peppers with olive oil.
2. **Cook the Filling:**
    - Heat olive oil in a large skillet over medium heat. Add the chopped onion and cook until softened, about 3-4 minutes.
    - Add the minced garlic and cook for another minute, until fragrant.
    - Add the ground meat to the skillet and cook until browned and fully cooked, breaking it up with a spoon as it cooks. Drain any excess fat if needed.
    - Stir in the cooked rice, diced tomatoes, tomato sauce, dried oregano, dried basil, paprika, salt, and pepper. Cook for another 2-3 minutes until well combined and heated through.
3. **Stuff the Peppers:**
    - Spoon the filling mixture into each bell pepper, packing it tightly.
    - Place the stuffed peppers upright in a baking dish. If there's leftover filling, you can spoon it around the peppers in the dish.
4. **Bake:**
    - Cover the baking dish with aluminum foil and bake in the preheated oven for 30 minutes.
    - Remove the foil, sprinkle the shredded cheese on top of each pepper, and bake uncovered for an additional 10-15 minutes, or until the peppers are tender and the cheese is melted and bubbly.
5. **Serve:**
    - Garnish with fresh parsley or basil if desired. Serve the stuffed peppers warm.

Tips:

- **Vegetarian Option:** Use cooked quinoa or additional beans in place of meat for a vegetarian version.
- **Extra Flavor:** Add some chopped olives or capers to the filling for a Mediterranean twist.
- **Make Ahead:** You can prepare the stuffed peppers a day in advance and store them in the refrigerator before baking. Add a few extra minutes to the baking time if baking from cold.
- **Freezing:** These stuffed peppers freeze well. After baking, let them cool completely, then freeze in an airtight container. Reheat from frozen in the oven at 350°F (175°C) until heated through.

Stuffed Bell Peppers are not only delicious but also allow for endless variations, making them a great addition to your meal rotation. Enjoy!

Peanut Butter and Banana Roll-Ups

Ingredients:

- 1 large tortilla (whole wheat, flour, or any preferred type)

- 2 tablespoons peanut butter (creamy or crunchy)
- 1 banana
- 1 tablespoon honey or maple syrup (optional, for extra sweetness)
- A sprinkle of cinnamon (optional)

Instructions:

1. **Prepare the Tortilla:**
    - Lay the tortilla flat on a clean surface or cutting board.
2. **Spread the Peanut Butter:**
    - Evenly spread the peanut butter over the entire surface of the tortilla, leaving a small border around the edges.
3. **Add Banana:**
    - Peel the banana and place it on one edge of the tortilla. You can slice the banana lengthwise or leave it whole, depending on your preference.
4. **Add Sweetener (Optional):**
    - Drizzle honey or maple syrup over the banana for added sweetness, if desired. Sprinkle a little cinnamon for extra flavor, if you like.
5. **Roll Up:**
    - Carefully roll the tortilla tightly from the edge with the banana to the opposite edge, ensuring it's wrapped snugly.
6. **Slice and Serve:**
    - Slice the roll-up into 1-inch pieces to make pinwheels, or cut it in half for a simple snack.

Tips:

- **Alternative Nut Butters:** You can substitute peanut butter with almond butter, cashew butter, or any other nut butter.
- **Add-ins:** Feel free to add a sprinkle of chia seeds, flaxseeds, or granola inside the roll-up for extra crunch and nutrition.
- **Fruit Variations:** Try using other fruits like strawberries, apples, or pears in place of bananas for different flavor combinations.

Peanut Butter and Banana Roll-Ups are a delightful, healthy option that's easy to customize and perfect for a quick snack or lunch!

Homemade Pizza Bagels

Ingredients:

- 4 plain bagels (or your favorite type)

- 1/2 cup pizza sauce or marinara sauce
- 1 cup shredded mozzarella cheese
- 1/2 cup grated Parmesan cheese (optional)
- 1/2 cup sliced pepperoni or other toppings (such as cooked sausage, mushrooms, bell peppers, olives, etc.)
- 1/2 teaspoon dried oregano
- 1/2 teaspoon dried basil
- 1/4 teaspoon garlic powder (optional)
- Fresh basil or parsley for garnish (optional)

Instructions:

1. **Preheat Oven:**
   - Preheat your oven to 375°F (190°C).
2. **Prepare Bagels:**
   - Slice the bagels in half and place them cut-side up on a baking sheet or oven-safe dish.
3. **Add Sauce:**
   - Spread a thin layer of pizza sauce or marinara sauce evenly over each bagel half.
4. **Add Cheese and Toppings:**
   - Sprinkle shredded mozzarella cheese generously over the sauce.
   - Add any additional toppings you like, such as sliced pepperoni, cooked sausage, or vegetables.
5. **Season:**
   - Sprinkle dried oregano, dried basil, and garlic powder (if using) over the top for added flavor.
6. **Bake:**
   - Bake in the preheated oven for 10-12 minutes, or until the cheese is melted and bubbly and the bagels are lightly toasted. For a crispier top, you can broil them for an additional 1-2 minutes, but watch them closely to avoid burning.
7. **Garnish and Serve:**
   - Remove from the oven and let cool slightly. Garnish with fresh basil or parsley if desired.
8. **Serve:**
   - Serve warm and enjoy!

Tips:

- **Customizable:** Feel free to customize your pizza bagels with your favorite toppings. You can also use a variety of cheeses or sauces.
- **Make-Ahead:** You can assemble the pizza bagels ahead of time and refrigerate them until you're ready to bake. Add a few extra minutes to the baking time if they are cold from the fridge.

- **Freezing:** To freeze, assemble the bagels, then wrap them individually in plastic wrap or foil and freeze. Bake directly from the freezer, adding a few extra minutes to the baking time.

Homemade Pizza Bagels are a versatile and delicious option that can be tailored to your taste preferences, making them a hit with both kids and adults!

Veggie-Packed Meatloaf

Ingredients:

- **For the Meatloaf:**
    - 1 pound (450 g) ground beef (or a mix of beef and pork)
    - 1/2 cup finely chopped onion
    - 1/2 cup finely chopped bell pepper (any color)
    - 1/2 cup finely chopped carrot
    - 1/2 cup finely chopped celery
    - 2 cloves garlic, minced
    - 1 cup breadcrumbs (Panko or regular)
    - 1/2 cup grated Parmesan cheese
    - 1 large egg
    - 1/2 cup milk
    - 1 tablespoon Worcestershire sauce
    - 1 teaspoon dried oregano
    - 1 teaspoon dried basil
    - Salt and pepper to taste
- **For the Glaze (optional):**
    - 1/4 cup ketchup
    - 2 tablespoons brown sugar
    - 1 tablespoon Dijon mustard

Instructions:

1. **Preheat Oven:**
    - Preheat your oven to 375°F (190°C). Lightly grease a loaf pan or line it with parchment paper.
2. **Prepare Vegetables:**
    - Finely chop the onion, bell pepper, carrot, and celery. You can use a food processor to speed up this process if you prefer.
3. **Cook Vegetables:**
    - In a skillet over medium heat, sauté the chopped vegetables and minced garlic in a little olive oil until softened, about 5-7 minutes. Let them cool slightly before adding them to the meat mixture.
4. **Mix Meatloaf:**
    - In a large bowl, combine the ground beef, sautéed vegetables, breadcrumbs, Parmesan cheese, egg, milk, Worcestershire sauce, dried oregano, dried basil, salt, and pepper. Mix until just combined, being careful not to overmix.
5. **Shape Meatloaf:**
    - Transfer the meat mixture to the prepared loaf pan and shape it into a loaf. Alternatively, you can shape it into a loaf on a baking sheet if you prefer a crustier exterior.
6. **Prepare Glaze (Optional):**
    - In a small bowl, mix together the ketchup, brown sugar, and Dijon mustard. Spread the glaze evenly over the top of the meatloaf.
7. **Bake:**

- Bake in the preheated oven for 45-55 minutes, or until the meatloaf reaches an internal temperature of 160°F (71°C) and is cooked through.
8. **Cool and Serve:**
    - Let the meatloaf rest for 10 minutes before slicing. This helps it hold its shape and makes it easier to slice.

Tips:

- **Customizable:** Feel free to use other vegetables like zucchini, mushrooms, or spinach. Just make sure they are finely chopped and cooked before adding them to the meat mixture.
- **Leftovers:** Veggie-Packed Meatloaf makes great leftovers. Store in an airtight container in the refrigerator for up to 4 days or freeze for up to 3 months.
- **Serving Suggestions:** Serve with mashed potatoes, steamed vegetables, or a simple salad for a complete meal.

Veggie-Packed Meatloaf is a delicious and nutritious twist on a classic dish, perfect for adding more veggies to your diet while enjoying a hearty meal.

Apple and Cheese Sandwiches

Ingredients:

- 2 slices of bread (whole wheat, sourdough, or your choice)
- 1 tablespoon mustard (Dijon or yellow, optional)
- 1 tablespoon mayonnaise or butter (optional)
- 1 apple (such as Fuji, Honeycrisp, or Granny Smith)
- 2-3 slices of cheese (cheddar, Swiss, or your favorite variety)
- Fresh spinach or arugula (optional)
- A drizzle of honey or a sprinkle of cinnamon (optional)

Instructions:

1. **Prepare the Apple:**
   - Wash and core the apple. Slice it into thin rounds or wedges. If you prefer, you can peel the apple before slicing, though the skin adds extra fiber and nutrients.
2. **Prepare the Bread:**
   - If desired, spread mustard and/or mayonnaise on one or both slices of bread for added flavor.
3. **Assemble the Sandwich:**
   - Lay out one slice of bread on a clean surface.
   - Place the cheese slices on top of the bread.
   - Arrange the apple slices evenly over the cheese.
   - If using, add a layer of fresh spinach or arugula on top of the apple slices.
4. **Finish and Serve:**
   - Top with the second slice of bread.
   - If you prefer, you can toast the sandwich in a skillet or a sandwich press for a warm, melted cheese effect. To do this, heat a skillet over medium heat, butter the outside of the sandwich if desired, and cook until golden brown and the cheese is melted, flipping once.
5. **Optional Add-Ons:**
   - Drizzle a small amount of honey over the apple slices or sprinkle with a touch of cinnamon for extra flavor before closing the sandwich.

Tips:

- **Cheese Choices:** Cheddar pairs well with apples for a sharp and tangy contrast, while Swiss or Gouda offers a milder, creamy flavor.
- **Bread Options:** Experiment with different types of bread such as whole grain, rye, or even a crusty baguette for varied textures.
- **Add-Ins:** For extra crunch, consider adding thin slices of cucumber or a handful of walnuts or pecans.
- **Serving Suggestions:** These sandwiches are great on their own or served with a side of salad or vegetable sticks.

Apple and Cheese Sandwiches offer a refreshing twist on traditional sandwiches and are perfect for a light meal or snack. Enjoy the combination of crisp apple and creamy cheese!